W9-AAW-399

THE GOOD, THE BAD, AND THE UGLY
PITTSBURGH STEELERS

HEART-POUNDING, JAW-DROPPING, AND GUT-WRENCHING MOMENTS FROM PITTSBURGH STEELERS HISTORY

Matt Fulks

TRIUMPH
BOOKS

Copyright © 2008 by Matt Fulks

No part of this publication may be reproduced, stored in a
retrieval system, or transmitted in any form by any means,
electronic, mechanical, photocopying, or otherwise, without
the prior written permission of the publisher, Triumph Books,
542 South Dearborn Street, Suite 750, Chicago, Illinois 60605.
Triumph Books and the colophon are registered trademarks
of Random House, Inc.

Library of Congress Cataloging-in-Publication Data

Fulks, Matt.
  The good, the bad, and the ugly : Pittsburgh Steelers heart-
pounding, jaw-dropping, and gut-wrenching moments from
Pittsburgh Steelers history / Matt Fulks.
      p. cm.
  Includes bibliographical references.
  ISBN-13: 978-1-57243-922-1
  ISBN-10: 1-57243-922-X
  1. Pittsburgh Steelers (Football team)—History. I. Title.
  GV956.P57F85 2008
  796.332'640974886—dc22
                                    2008021093

This book is available in quantity at special discounts for your
group or organization. For further information, contact:

Triumph Books
542 South Dearborn Street
Suite 750
Chicago, Illinois 60605
(312) 939-3330
Fax (312) 663-3557

Printed in U.S.A.
ISBN: 978-1-57243-922-1
All photos courtesy of AP Images except where otherwise noted.

Content packaged by Mojo Media, Inc.
Joe Funk: Editor
Jason Hinman: Creative Director

Designed by Patricia Frey

To my family—my wife, Libby, and our kids, Helen, Charlie, and Aaron. Thanks for your support and for putting up with my Elvis habits. I love you.

CONTENTS

FOREWORD

When someone says "Pittsburgh Steelers," one of the first things I think about is "the Chief"—Art Rooney and the rest of the Rooney family, and the tradition of winning they built with this organization. Besides the fact that they're a genuinely great family, the Rooneys built a franchise that evolved from perennial losers to a dynasty. More important, they built a franchise that has had a huge impact on the people of the blue-collar working town of Pittsburgh.

It was a tremendous honor to represent the people of Pittsburgh as a member of the Steelers. When the Steelers drafted me out of Notre Dame in 1968, there weren't a lot of expectations on either side. They were seen as the "same old Steelers," the team that hadn't won much during the 1960s. And they didn't take a huge chance on me, considering they took me in the 16th round. Not a lot was expected of a 5'11" running back.

That first year, 1968, the Steelers went 2–11–1. As you'll read about later in this book, I wouldn't play for the Steelers again for four seasons. Near the end of 1968, I received my draft notice for Vietnam. After being wounded in Heip Duc, it looked like any hope I had of an NFL career was over.

My comeback, and becoming a productive member of the Steelers again in 1972, largely goes back to the Rooney family. The Chief was willing to give me a chance to work my way onto the roster. For that, and for being the best owner in the league, I'll forever be grateful to the Chief and the entire Rooney family.

One of the best moves the Rooney family made was the hiring of Chuck Noll as head coach. Bringing in Chuck in 1969, a year before the team moved into Three Rivers Stadium, was really a new start for the franchise. They came into their own about the same time. The difference between Chuck and previous coaches, such as my first coach, Bill Austin, is what Chuck brought to the team. He brought the values of the Rooney family.

Chuck was a good man and an excellent coach. He brought a philosophy and an image of how he saw things that ultimately created a dynasty. I really believe that was a big part of it. Previous coaches had been around, but none of them really identified themselves with Pittsburgh. However, this was Chuck's first coaching job, so he was willing to build the program; he drafted many players who emerged as great talents. He wanted members of the Steelers to be Steelers from day one. So our success in the 1970s—and, frankly, beyond—came from a combination of those things surrounding Chuck Noll.

Of course, the players didn't respond to Chuck immediately. As with any coaching change, there are turning points. We had to buy into the philosophy and the coach and the direction. That became a personal thing. It wasn't as if we looked around, saw a wonderful team, and collectively decided that we were a championship-caliber team. Each individual had to be willing to do his part and sacrifice for the betterment of others and for the whole of the team. It wasn't until I helped contribute to the success of the team that I felt I was a true part of this organization. That's the way it is for players in most team sports. As an athlete, a competitor, you want to feel as if the team is counting on you to win.

Ultimately for me, as for many of us, the turning point came during the "Immaculate Reception" in the playoff game against the Raiders in 1972. It gave us the belief that we could win big games. Some people point to the win against the Raiders in the 1974 playoffs. But for many of us it was the 1972 game, because after 40 years of losing, we finally won a big game—and on a miracle play, no less. It was almost as if the football gods had finally changed their minds about us. Even though we lost the following week to Miami, we had reached a big turning point. Suddenly we had some success. In '73, we tried to build on it. We played well and reached the playoffs, but we weren't quite over the next hurdle.

Then, in '74, we beat the Raiders in Oakland and were headed to our first Super Bowl. Talk about wanting to be a part of a team's success. Everyone's watching the Super Bowl, so as a player, you want to do everything possible to be at your best. For the most part, we were.

Each member of those teams has been asked if he had a favorite Super Bowl. For me, each one has a story. Each one was different. Super Bowl IX was the first one. Frankly, who would've known at that point that there'd be others? But there were. The second one, Super Bowl X, against Dallas, is best remembered for Lynn Swann, who came up big in that game. In Super Bowl X, star power, which we had developed through the draft, helped us.

To return in Super Bowl XIII, and to beat Dallas again in a remarkable game, was unique. Then, the fourth one, Super Bowl XIV. There was a lot of pressure on us because of the expectations. We were 11-point favorites. The Los Angeles Rams were a 9–7 team playing in their hometown with basically no pressure. We had a lot riding on that one. It turned out to be a sloppy game, but we won.

Those last two Super Bowls, in my perspective, were the most fun because I felt that no one could beat us. We had come of age. We had enough experience that we were the big kids on the block. And we ran over everybody. If we lost it was because we beat ourselves. In both of those games, the only way we wouldn't have won the championship was if we screwed up. The Cowboys and the Rams weren't going to dominate us.

You'll read extensively about Chuck Noll and each of those four Super Bowls in *The Good, the Bad, and the Ugly: Pittsburgh Steelers.* You'll also read about our defensive coordinator, the man behind the Steel Curtain, Bud Carson.

At that time in the NFL—and we still see it today—a defense will go into its game plan and stick with it, oftentimes a safe defense like a cover two. Bud Carson, though, would audible the defense, much like a quarterback does on offense. Bud would change his defense on a play and then if the offense changed, he would change back.

All of a sudden you start to have some success and get a swagger and then you start to believe. We believed, on offense and defense.

Besides all of the great successes we've had with this organization, including Super Bowl XL, in *The Good, the Bad, and the Ugly: Pittsburgh Steelers* you'll get a chance to learn about some of those failures during the team's first 40 years. You'll read about some of the great characters who have called Pittsburgh home, including Bill Dudley, Ernie Stautner, and Bill Cowher. And, of course, you'll read about some of the moments that have been tough for all Steelers fans, such as some off-the-field struggles, how the team got rid of two Hall of Fame quarterbacks in the 1950s, the 1976 team (which could've won another Super Bowl if we hadn't suffered a couple injuries before the AFC championship), and the 1994 playoff loss to San Diego.

Author Matt Fulks stressed to me a few times during the writing of *The Good, the Bad, and the Ugly: Pittsburgh Steelers* that this is not intended to be a complete history of the Pittsburgh Steelers. And it's not. However, through the good—and in spite of the bad and the ugly—this book reminds us why we're proud to be Pittsburgh Steelers.

—Rocky Bleier

ACKNOWLEDGMENTS

One of Keith Jackson's former statisticians, Mike Swanson, told me a story while I was writing this book about how he screwed up some stats that he handed to Jackson during the broadcast of the 1980 South Carolina–Georgia football game. Seemingly in spite of the mistakes, Jackson still credited Swanson on the air during the game's closing moments. Afterward, Swanson asked Jackson, "Why did you mention my name today? I was awful." Jackson replied, "That's why. I wanted the whole world to know who did the stats today." Although it would take me a Keith Jackson broadcast to thank everyone who played a part in what you're about to read, and any screwups you might read are entirely my fault, I want the whole world to know that the following were instrumental:

To Mike Emmerich, Don Gulbrandsen, Tom Bast, and the rest of the team at Triumph Books for giving me the opportunity to write about the favorite NFL team of my childhood, and for the patience and restraint they showed as we got closer to (and ultimately passed) the deadline.

To all of the men and women who have covered the Steelers over the years for newspapers, magazines, and book projects, I'm grateful.

This will seem like an odd thanks, but I want to thank every Steelers fan—and others—who contributed some type of video to YouTube. It's pretty amazing to think that in minutes you can access complete game videos or at least certain plays, instead of relying solely on what other writers describe.

To Rocky Bleier, for writing the foreword and offering some great stories. To Andy Russell, for taking time for an interview about his years with the team, which started with the "SOS" teams and ended during the glory years. I also owe a thanks to former Steelers I've interviewed in the past, most notably for the book *Super Bowl Sunday*: Dwight White, Woody Widenhofer, and Matt Bahr.

To lifelong Pittsburgh resident Tim Conn, his mother, Mary Louise, and his brother, Billy, a special thanks for the memories of Art Rooney and for the tour of Pittsburgh. To my agent, Rob Wilson, who patiently put our project on hold while I finished this book. To Pittsburgh native and longtime WDAF-TV (Kansas City) sports director Frank Boal, for offering personal contacts.

To John Sprugel at Metro Sports, for working around a couple of article deadlines while I finished this book.

To Dave and Kathy Minich, for giving me a hideaway in the middle of Missouri so I could work on this project.

To the group of friends and family who serve as my core support and guidance, I owe a mountain of gratitude: Steve Treece, Dave O'Hara, Jim Wissel, and Tom Lawrence. Plus Tim and Amy Brown, who were a source of endless encouragement and stress relief during the entire project. Your friendship is appreciated more than I'll ever show. I have to add that I prayed a lot during this project, particularly the last few weeks. I felt like a slow quarterback going up against the Steel Curtain. Without Christ this isn't possible. A final special thanks to my favorite in-laws, Todd and Pat Burwell; and my parents, Fred and Sharon, who served as encouragers and babysitters. To my best friend, Libby, who kept her sanity when I lost mine; and our three children, Helen, Charlie, and Aaron, who were subjected to more *Scooby-Doo* and *Word World* episodes than any one child should be in a lifetime, but they love me anyway.

Thank you all.

INTRODUCTION

I'm from Kansas City. That's not meant as a proud statement—although I am proud of that fact—or a statement in search of sympathy. Rather, I'm stating that to help explain how I got here as a potential bandwagon fan.

In spite of my Kansas City roots, I grew up as a die-hard Steelers fan. See, the Chiefs of my youth were wretched. Similar to some of the Steelers teams you'll read about on the following pages. Although I wanted to see the Chiefs win, at the age of five years old I wanted to latch on to a good team.

Of course, in the mid-1970s, that team was the Pittsburgh Steelers. At least it seemed obvious to me that it was the Steelers. Several of my buddies fell in love with those detestable Cowboys, who somehow had been crowned as "America's Team." I've never figured that one out.

As a child I can't remember how many times I practiced an acrobatic Lynn Swann catch in the front yard, pretending my dad was Terry Bradshaw. Man, I wanted to be Swann in the worst way. It didn't take long to realize that I didn't have the speed, grace, athleticism, and just plain natural God-given ability that Swann possessed, but I didn't let that stop me. I'd still bundle up in my Steelers jacket and stocking cap in the dead of winter, drag Dad outside with me, and try to make those diving catches.

You might have a similar memory. That's just the way it was with this new phenomenon of "Steeler Nation." The Steelers were everywhere nationally. We heard Rocky Bleier's story and instantly became fans. We saw "Mean" Joe Greene toss his jersey to the "kid" and, strangely, we wanted Mean Joe to toss us a sweaty jersey too.

So, since I became hooked when the Steelers were good, and I've never lived in Pittsburgh, I guess you can call me a bandwagon fan. (Although I'm not sure I knew any better in kindergarten.) I eventually learned that no matter how bad the Chiefs played, since they're in my hometown, I have to pull for them. But I haven't hopped off the Steelers' bandwagon. Even though I no longer have the Steelers jacket or stocking cap, and you won't find Steelers posters and pictures thumbtacked to my bedroom walls, I've stuck with the team, including the Mark Malone and Bubby Brister eras, and then back to the championship-caliber teams under Bill Cowher.

Many of those players and teams that I fell in love with as a child are represented on the following pages. Not all, but many, because *The Good, the Bad, and the Ugly: Pittsburgh Steelers* isn't meant to be a complete history of the organization. Frankly, I admire the men who have tried to do that. What a daunting task to put together a book about the history of this organization in just a couple hundred pages.

This book covers many of the more important players and moments throughout the Steelers' history, which hit 75 years in 2007—the team's inception, many of the Hall of Famers, and, of course, the Super Bowls. But it also highlights some of the forgotten players and moments that have made this a great organization. And, as the title suggests, it also hits some of the lower moments the organization has gone through. Every team in every professional sport has some skeletons in their closets, including the Steelers. They can't—and really shouldn't—be avoided.

There are great moments and players that you won't find here. Or you might just see their names mentioned briefly. For instance, you won't see a lot of ink on men like Johnny "Blood" McNally or Bobby Layne or L.C. Greenwood or Louis Lipps. As important as each of those players has been—not to mention countless other players—simply put, this book might best be considered a snapshot of the team's history.

Another player who isn't covered significantly in this book is Ernie Holmes, a member of the Steel Curtain. Sadly, Holmes, who was known for years by his arrowhead haircut, died in a car accident in Texas three days before this book was completed. Holmes, who had gone into the ministry, was not wearing his seat belt at the time of the single-car accident. He was 59.

Throughout the pages of this book, you'll also read about some of the great rivals, such as Cleveland, Cincinnati, and Oakland, along with classic matchups with Baltimore and the New York Giants.

Speaking of rivalries, during the writing of the book, someone emailed the following joke to me out of the blue. As with most jokes, this one might be as old as the team itself, so the author is unknown. But it's worth retelling.

Once upon a time—long, long ago—there was a season when neither the Browns nor the Steelers made the postseason playoffs. It seemed so unusual that the management of both teams got together and decided there should be some sort of competition between the two teams because of their great rivalry. So they decided on a week-long ice fishing competition. Of course, the team with the most fish at the end of the week would win.

So on a cold, freezing day on Lake Erie they began their contest. At the end of the first day, after eight hours of fishing the Browns had caught no fish and the Steelers had 100.

At the end of the second day, the Browns had caught no fish and the Steelers had 200.

That evening the Browns' coach got his team together and said, "I suspect some kind of cheating is taking place."

So the next morning, he dressed one of his players in black and gold and sent him over to the Steelers camp to act as a spy. At the end of the day the spy came back to report to the coach. The coach asked, "Well, how about it, are they cheating?"

"They sure are," the player reported. "They're cutting holes in the ice!"

This book, by and large, is about the people, games, and moments that have made the Pittsburgh Steelers organization what it is today. And in a small way it reminds us—young and old, bandwagon or Pittsburgh native—why we're a part of Steeler Nation.

Matt Fulks
January 2008

THE GOOD

THE "CHIEF" AND THE START OF A FRANCHISE

A "man's man." Ladies, that's not a phrase guys throw around willy-nilly. (But then again, neither is "willy-nilly.") In a guy's vernacular, saying someone is a man's man means the utmost respect.

Art Rooney was a man's man.

Not a man's man in the Pittsburgh boxer Billy Conn sort of way. Rooney wasn't built like a Greek god and he didn't have leading-man good looks. In fact, an article from *Time* magazine in 1937 described Rooney as looking "a great deal like a football himself." But in his younger days Rooney was an athlete, excelling in multiple sports. As he grew older, he knew how to bet on horses. He started a pro franchise. He was humble and generous. He even chomped on cigars. Simply put: guys admired Art Rooney.

Rooney was known by such nicknames as the Chief, the Old Man, or the Prez.

"He was a man who belonged to the entire world of sports," the late commissioner Pete Rozelle said upon Rooney's death in 1988. "It is questionable whether any sports figure was more universally loved and respected."

During his formidable years, Rooney was quite an athlete. Knute Rockne offered him a football scholarship to Notre Dame—twice—but Rooney turned him down. As a baseball player, he had been offered contracts by the Chicago Cubs and the Boston Red Sox. He signed with Boston for $250 a month, but realized he

Art Rooney, president of the Steelers, poses with his son Dan, general manager of the club, in Pittsburgh, in January 1966.

could make more money playing with barnstorming teams. So he did that for more than 15 years.

Rooney's real skill came inside the ring. He was an outstanding boxer in a town that was a hotbed for the sport through the first half of the 20th century. Pittsburgh produced the likes of world champions Harry Greb, Conn, and Fritzie Zivic. Rooney might've been right there with them. He won the AAU welterweight crown, and he was invited to represent the United States at the 1920 Olympics in Antwerp. Besides his mother not liking the idea, Rooney was heavily involved with other ventures, so he turned down the offer. (Incidentally, the fighter who went in his place and won a gold medal was named Sammy Mosberg. Rooney beat Mosberg shortly before and after the Games.)

Rooney also had an early penchant for team management. Before starting the Steelers in 1933, he had played on and ran several semipro football teams, including one he started as a teenager called the Hope-Harveys That team's games drew as many as 12,000 people and became a fan favorite. There were also Majestic Radio and James P. Rooney teams.

In the summer of 1933, the NFL was looking to expand. Pittsburgh had been on the radar but the NFL hadn't gone there because of the Pennsylvania "blue laws," which, among other things, prohibited organized leagues from playing on Sunday. With the blue laws about to be repealed, NFL commissioner Joe Carr talked to Rooney about buying a team.

Rooney dove into the NFL for the miniscule amount of $2,500—a mighty sum during the Depression era. It's long been thought and assumed that Rooney used his winnings from a big day at the track with Giants founder Tim Mara to buy the team. Rooney's son Dan calls that story nonsense, because his father already had the money to afford the NFL fee, even during those times, and because the Chief's record day at the track didn't happen until 1936.

"When he was lucky and did have winning times [betting on horses], that did help keep the team going," Dan Rooney said. "I might also say that my father promoted fights, and strangely enough as this would sound now, the fights that were promoted carried the football. Because I will tell you that the Steelers lost money every year. They came in [the league] in 1933 and they did not make money until 1946."

The Pittsburgh Pirates, named after their baseball counterpart, featured many of the players from the James P. Rooney club.

Although the Pirates didn't take the league by storm in their first year, their 3–6–2 record in 1933 under head coach Jap Douds was respectable. That was enough for players then. Football, even professional football, remained more of a hobby back then. It was a chance for most guys to keep their passion for the game.

"In those days, nobody got wealthy in sports," Rooney said. "You had two thrills. One came Sunday, trying to win the game. The next came Monday, trying to make the payroll."

It would be a long time before the Pirates, who became the Steelers in 1941, resembled anything close to a good team. Their closest in the early years came in 1936, when they finished with a .500 record, 6–6.

"Then I made a mistake," Rooney told the *Pittsburgh Post-Gazette* in 1964. "I let [head coach Joe] Bach go to Niagara University. If he had stayed here, we might have won our share of championships."

Instead, the team's first winning season wouldn't come until 1942, when Pittsburgh finished 7–4.

Rooney, who grew up the eldest of nine children to Margaret and Daniel Rooney, a saloon keeper on Pittsburgh's North Side—at the exact site where Three Rivers Stadium would eventually be placed—always had a love for both sports and Pittsburgh.

So, no matter how badly the team performed on the field, he had no desire to desert his hometown. Several times during the early days of the team when it struggled to be competitive, Rooney had offers to move the team to other cities. He turned each offer down, saying Pittsburgh was home.

The closest he ever came to leaving was in 1940. The franchise was losing a ton of money, so Rooney sold the Steelers to Boston businessman Lex Thompson, who wanted to move the team to Boston. Then Rooney bought half of the Philadelphia Eagles from his friend Bert Bell. They were going to split games 50–50 between Pittsburgh and Philadelphia. After the sales went through, several owners blocked the Steelers' move to Boston. So Rooney, Bell, and Thompson worked out a deal where they swapped franchises, which put Rooney back in Pittsburgh as part owner, along with Bell.

Rooney didn't like to hear people talk about how bad his Steelers were during the team's first four decades because he desperately wanted to win. But as much as anything, the NFL team gave him a chance to stay out of a mill and involved in sports. And around the track. Rooney, who eventually owned horse-racing tracks in Pennsylvania and New York and a 350-acre breeding farm in Maryland, loved to bet on the horses. Not only that, he was great at it.

"For a period of years after 1927 I was one of the country's biggest and most successful horseplayers," Rooney said in 1964, the year he was inducted into the Pro Football Hall of Fame. "I'm still considered one of the top handicappers in the country.... And I never have made as much as a $2 bet at any track I had an interest in."

Rooney never changed throughout his life. He walked to the stadium nearly every day. He remained generous with his winnings at the track. He lived in the same house throughout his adult life. And he always wanted whatever was best for the NFL and for his players.

Regardless of the era, one constant with Rooney, win or lose at the track or on the field, was the family atmosphere he fostered in the organization. He cared about each player individually. Obviously, his sons were an integral part of the organization throughout its history. But he saw the players as sons too.

"The Chief was a very interesting man and a definite class act," said Andy Russell, who gave Rooney the game ball from Super Bowl IX. "He would come down to the field for practices. The weather didn't matter. He was just a great guy to play for. He's the one who taught us to give back to the community."

"When he shook your hand," Joe Greene said of Rooney, "he put it in there and he kept it in there and let you feel it. He didn't put it and take it out. He didn't talk to you and look away, not look you in the eye. And he did that when he walked through the community—his community—talking to each and every [person]."

The players felt so endeared to Rooney that, as one story goes, one Christmas, Terry Bradshaw, Lynn Swann, and their wives stood outside the Rooney house and sang Christmas carols. Can you imagine many owners today evoking that type of response from their players?

"He was always so happy and jovial, a man with a very gracious personality and many flattering comments," Bradshaw wrote in his book, *Looking Deep,* of getting to know Rooney early in his career. "The full impact didn't hit me then, but soon I would grow to realize that I'd never meet another person like Mr. Rooney."

On August 25, 1988, Arthur Joseph Rooney died from complications following a stroke he had suffered on August 17 at his office. He was 87.

ERNIE STAUTNER: STEEL CITY TOUGH

One word describes Ernie Stautner: tough as steel. Okay, that's three words, but Ernie Stautner deserves however many descriptions for "tough" that are out there.

"Anybody that played in my era would say that Ernie Stautner was probably the toughest tackle that ever played," said Dante Lavelli, a Hall of Fame end for the Cleveland Browns during 1946–56. "And to me, Ernie Stautner was really a symbol of a defensive tackle."

Over a 14-season career, 1950–63, a time when the Steeler teams (for the most part) weren't very good, Stautner, the team's second-round draft pick, became the face of the organization. In those 14 years, thanks mainly to an inept offense and a rotation of coaches, the Steelers produced only four winning seasons: 1958, '59, '62, and '63.

The true saving grace for those Pittsburgh teams was the defense, which would leave opponents black and blue. Stautner represented everything good and rough about the team's bone-crushing image.

"His face, emerging directly from his shoulder without the benefit of a neck, is about as pretty as an auto accident," Myron Cope wrote in an article for *True* magazine in September 1964. "His philosophy is simple, if chilling, 'You got to be a man who wants to hurt somebody. You know where I'm going for? The quarterback's face. It hurts in the face. I want him to know I'm coming the next time. I want him to be scared. Those quarterbacks can't tell me they don't scare, because I've seen it in the corners of their eyes.'"

Stautner played hurt often. He was known to have broken ribs, a broken nose, bum shoulder, and numerous cuts and scrapes. One time he fractured his finger during a defensive series. He simply taped it and kept playing, never missing a down. In fact, Stautner missed only six games during his entire career.

As a testament to his dominance in spite of the wretched teams, Stautner was selected for nine Pro Bowl teams, which was the most for a Steeler until Joe Greene reached his ninth 17 years later.

Ernie Stautner, whose family immigrated to the United States from Germany in 1928 when he was about 3, really shouldn't have been playing football, especially at a Hall of Fame level.

He was seen as too small, at 6'1" and 230 pounds, especially for a defensive tackle or defensive end, even in the 1950s. He even ended up playing collegiate ball at Boston College, in essence because the coaches at Notre Dame didn't think he was big enough to play in college. That tag followed him to the pros. He had hoped to be drafted by the New York Giants, but they thought he was too small.

And if it had been up to his dad, Stautner wouldn't have pursued football in the first place. When Ernie was in elementary school in Albany, New York, he hurt his ankles and had to see a doctor. Since his parents, who couldn't speak a lick of English, were doing all they could to make it in Depression-era America, Ernie's dad told him: "Keine mehr Fußball. Keine mehr yamerung." Translated, that basically means: "No more football. No more complaining." Of course, Ernie Stautner—with his German stubbornness—continued to play football without his parents' knowledge. After all, they couldn't read or understand English. That is, until Stautner was an all-city selection as a senior in high school. The accolade included his photo in the Albany newspaper.

"What could he do then but be proud?" Ernie Stautner said, when asked about his dad's reaction.

When he was 17, Stautner joined the Marines and fought in the battle of Okinawa during World War II.

Besides his reputation for being tough, Stautner was extremely quick and possessed powerful forearms that defenders often felt crushing their heads

"That man ain't human," said Baltimore Colts Hall of Fame lineman Jim Parker. "He's too strong to be human. He's the toughest guy in the league to play against because he keeps coming head first. Swinging those forearms wears you down. That animal used to stick his head in my belly and drive me into the backfield so hard that, when I picked myself up and looked around, there was a path chopped through the field like a farmer had run a plow over it."

In 1964, a year after Stautner retired from the Steelers, the team retired his No. 70. Today it remains the only number the team has honored that way.

After a long career in coaching, Stautner, who was a first-ballot Hall of Famer in 1969, retired to the Aspen, Colorado, area. In February 2006, he died in Carbondale, Colorado, due to complications from Alzheimer's disease. He was 80.

"MEAN" JOE WHO?

The Steelers had been pitiful for nearly the entire decade of the 1960s. In 1968, Pittsburgh allowed more points (397) than any other team in the NFL.

Heading into the 1969 NFL draft, the Steelers had won 11 games—over their previous three seasons. During that same three-year span, tiny North Texas State had lost only five contests and had won the Missouri Valley Conference title two times.

The Steelers needed help on the field. It seemed they needed some help in their scouting department as well. The draft, particularly first- or second-round picks, just hadn't been kind to Pittsburgh.

There were Mike Taylor and Ernie Ruple in 1968. The two spent a combined three seasons with the Steelers. Don Shy in '67. Dick Leftridge in '66. Not exactly draft excellence.

But under first-year head coach Chuck Noll, the Steelers were ready to make amends with their first pick (fourth overall) in 1969. After O.J. Simpson (Buffalo), George Kunz (Atlanta), and Leroy Keyes (Philadelphia) were selected, Pittsburgh shocked everyone by choosing All-American Joe Greene, a relatively unknown defensive tackle from North Texas State.

Steeler fans weren't amused. The feeling was mutual for Greene, who was 6'4" and 275 pounds.

"I didn't think it was a great day for me," Greene said of being picked by the Steelers. "Pittsburgh hadn't won any ballgames. Pittsburgh wasn't one of the best football teams—if they weren't

Joe Greene swoops in on Cowboys fullback Walt Garrison, in Irving, Texas, in October 1972.

at the bottom, they were very close, for a long, long, long time."

The old joke—the one you'll read about in nearly every story about Greene—is the reaction of Steelers fans, as well as the media, when Pittsburgh made Greene its first pick in 1969: "Who's Joe Greene?" It was a legitimate question. After all, without 24-hour sports channels and Internet chat rooms, people in Pittsburgh didn't know about this dominating lineman from a small Texas school. (Who are we kidding? There probably were some football fans in Texas who didn't know the name Joe Greene.)

That sentiment wasn't reserved only for people outside of the organization though. The players wondered the same thing.

"MEAN" JOE GREENE

91—Consecutive games played, 1969–75.
16—Career fumble recoveries.
11—Career-high number of sacks in 1972.
10—Pro Bowl appearances.
5—Sacks against Houston in 1972.
2—NFL Defensive Player of the Year awards (1972 and '74).
1—Steelers draft pick in 1969.

"There was a lot of cynicism by the veterans over draft picks who failed," said Andy Russell, who was a veteran linebacker in 1969. "All of a sudden they drafted a guy we'd never heard of. There were thoughts that the Steelers just wasted another draft pick. Then Joe held out for more money and showed up to camp a day late. That didn't help."

It didn't take long, however, before everyone from fans and the media to cynical veterans—opponents included—found out who this Joe Greene was.

When Greene showed up for his first day of practice, the Steelers were running a drill they called "Oklahoma." Teams have different names for the drill, but basically it's where a defensive lineman is trying to get to the running back. Of course, the defensive lineman first has to get past his offensive counterpart. Much like in a game, the drill is slightly easier for the offensive lineman because he knows the snap count.

The veterans were eager to take on this rookie, who was not only unknown to them but also had held out for a bigger contract. Longtime center Ray Mansfield jumped in there first to block the team's top draft pick.

"Big mistake," Russell said with a chuckle. "Joe just picked him up and moved him out of the way. The next guy was Bruce Van Dyke, who ultimately was a Pro Bowl guard. Joe threw him away. We knew we finally had somebody. Joe was unblockable. Other teams didn't know what to do with him. He was unbelievable."

TRIVIA

Had the Steelers not traded him when they drafted Joe Greene, what veteran player would've played behind the outstanding rookie Greene?

Find the answers on pages 165–166.

During Greene's rookie season, it seemed like the Steelers didn't really know what to do with him either. Stories about his temper (or his aggressiveness, however you see it)—kicking opponents, stepping on opponents, smacking opponents—throughout his career have become legendary. He even spit in the face of Dick Butkus, the equally intense Chicago Bear. "Joe doesn't like to admit he did that," Russell says, "but I saw him do it."

In spite of the poor team around him and his tirades and ejections, Greene was selected as the NFL's Rookie of the Year in 1969. It would be one of many awards and accolades handed to Greene during his 13-year playing career.

In 1972, the Steelers took a 9–3 record into Houston to face the 1–11 Oilers. It turned out to be one of Greene's signature games.

With two regular-season contests remaining, Pittsburgh needed a win to wrap up the division championship for the first time and secure a spot in the playoffs, also for the first time. There was just one problem: injuries. The Steelers sideline looked more like a scene from *ER*.

According to a story on the Steelers website, "L.C. Greenwood and Sam Davis were out. Jon Kolb and Gerry Mullins had the flu; while Kolb played, Mullins only made it into the third quarter. Bruce Van Dyke pulled a calf muscle in the first quarter and was done for the day; Jim Clack injured an ankle and was done for the day. Craig Hanneman, Greenwood's backup, aggravated a knee injury and was done for the day; Dwight White injured a knee; Steve Furness injured an ankle. Ron Shanklin was injured in the first quarter and was done for the day; Terry Bradshaw dislocated a finger in the second quarter and was done for the day; and tight end Larry Brown, who would grow into an offensive tackle, was that day playing flanker."

In other words, even though the Steelers were facing the one-win Oilers, Houston certainly had a better chance of picking up its

TRIVIA

What's the largest number of Steelers who have received Pro Bowl honors in the same year? And in what year(s)?

Find the answers on pages 165–166.

second win. That is, if it weren't for Joe Greene.

Greene essentially placed Pittsburgh on his back and dominated Houston's offense. He finished the day with five sacks, a forced fumble, a fumble recovery, and he blocked a short field-goal attempt. The Steelers won 9–3. Incidentally, those two fumbles that Greene had his hand in resulted in two of Roy Gerela's three field goals.

The Steelers indeed reached the playoffs that season, eventually losing to Miami—the undefeated Dolphins—in the AFC Championship Game.

With the addition of "Mean" Joe Greene in 1969, along with subsequent drafts that included other integral building blocks, the Steelers turned into football's greatest dynasty of the 1970s and solidified themselves as one of the best pro football organizations of all time.

In 1987, because of his supremacy and longevity, Greene was elected to the Pro Football Hall of Fame. He was the first player from the dynasty years to be elected to the hall. Nine more have followed, including Noll.

Since his playing career ended in 1981, Greene has been a television analyst for CBS Sports and an assistant line coach for the Steelers, Dolphins, and Cardinals. In 2004 he became a special assistant for college and pro personnel for the Steelers.

By the way, in case you're wondering why Greene is the only player from the Steelers dynasty featured in this chapter, Andy Russell probably provides the best answer.

"Joe Greene is unquestionably the player of the decade for the NFL in the 1970s," Russell said when asked if Greene is the ultimate Steeler. "No player did more for his team than Joe Greene for the Steelers.... He turned us around. You don't do that single-handedly, of course, but Joe created the path for our winning."

Although it's not officially retired, no other Steeler has worn No. 75 since Greene.

COKE GIVES GREENE A NEW REPUTATION

Yes, Joe Greene was known as "Mean." And yes, he lived up to that reputation on the field. But he always contended that he wasn't really that menacing of a figure. The public started to believe Greene in 1979 when he starred in the popular commercial for Coca-Cola's new "Coke Adds Life" campaign. Several times over it's been ranked as one of the greatest commercials of all time.

Greene and the 12-year-old boy, Tommy Okon, a veteran commercial actor, spent two 18-hour days shooting the commercial in New Rochelle, New York. Greene drank about a case of Coke during those two days.

Originally, Coca-Cola executives picked Dallas quarterback Roger Staubach to star opposite Okon. However, the advertising agency, McCann-Erickson, wanted to use Greene and his gruff persona. Greene nearly declined. In fact, when he was first approached, Greene simply replied, "Hell no!"

"I've always striven to be the best," he said years later. "I didn't want to fall on my face as an actor."

He definitely didn't. The spot won two 1979 CLIO awards, advertising's top honors, including the best actor nod going to Greene.

"I really think it humanized a guy who had been dehumanized a little bit," Greene said. "I had a reputation as a mean guy, and it carried over off the field. I was somewhat unapproachable. Then the commercial portrayed me as a big pussycat."

In 1981, there was a television movie, *The Steeler and the Pittsburgh Kid*, based on the commercial and the lives of Greene and "the kid." However, Okon was thought to be too big to play himself, so Henry Thomas played the part. (Thomas later starred opposite the alien in *E.T.*)

Although it wasn't his intent, the commercial did paint Greene in a completely different light. And it made thousands of kids around the country dream of the day they could exchange a bottle of Coke for a sweaty Mean Joe Greene jersey.

DID YOU KNOW...

Pro football was born in Pittsburgh? It's generally believed that the Pittsburgh Athletic Club and the Allegheny Athletic Association played each other on November 12, 1892, at Recreation Park in Pittsburgh. Up until that point, players willingly played for free. But the Allegheny Athletic Association paid former Yale All-American guard William "Pudge" Heffelfinger $500. Adding fuel to this playing-for-free fire, according to the Pro Football Hall of Fame, the PAC had offered Heffelfinger $250 to play in the game, but he wasn't willing to risk his amateur status for such an amount. When the Allegheny team found this out, they signed Heffelfinger for double the Pittsburgh club's offer.

THE STEELERS' MOST IMPORTANT WIN OF ALL TIME

When you're talking about an organization that is one of only three in NFL history with five Super Bowl rings, not to mention countless "important" games, picking one might seem absurd. But it isn't as crazy or difficult as you think. The one that stands out above the others, the one that really set up the franchise for a dynasty in the 1970s, is the 1974 AFC Championship Game between the Steelers and the Oakland Raiders.

By 1974, the Steelers and the Raiders had a great rivalry. The teams hated each other—although most teams hated the Raiders then. Each team had won a playoff game against the other during the previous two seasons, and they had also been playing each other during the regular season.

As much as the Steelers had improved during the early part of the decade, they were looking for their first statement game, which would mean reaching the Super Bowl.

After cruising through the regular season with a 10–3–1 record, and having very little trouble against Buffalo in an AFC playoff game, winning 32–14, the Steelers would have to go through Oakland to win their first AFC title.

Getty Images

Lynn Swann catches a touchdown pass from Terry Bradshaw during the 1974 AFC Championship Game against the Oakland Raiders on December 29, 1974, in Oakland. The Steelers won 24–13.

Oakland, which was boasting a 12–2 record, was coming off an emotional last-minute win against defending Super Bowl champs Miami in their AFC playoff contest. With the Dolphins as good as they were and the Raiders being one of the elite teams in the AFC, the game turned out to be as exciting as people expected. Miami scored late in the fourth quarter, taking a 26–21 lead. But then Ken Stabler drove the Raiders down the field and into the end zone during the final few seconds. Oakland won 28–26.

Afterward, Miami guard Larry Little said, "The two best teams in football played today." Raider coach John Madden didn't disagree.

"When the best plays the best," he said, "anything can happen."

So where did that leave the Steelers? Not very happy and a little

TRIVIA

What was the outcome of the first-ever Steelers game in 1933?

Find the answers on pages 165-166.

more motivated. When Chuck Noll met Tuesday with his team for the first time since that week before the Oakland game, he wasn't happy.

"They say the best two teams played [Sunday] in Oakland," Noll, who wasn't a rah-rah kind of coach, growled to his team. "Well, they're not the best. The best team is in *this* locker room!"

One of Pittsburgh's three losses that season came against the Raiders. And it wasn't even close, 17–0 at home. So maybe the Raiders felt they had a reason to be somewhat confident. After Noll's speech—combined with ire over Madden's comments—the Steelers' unshakable will manifested itself.

"We were determined to win this one," said linebacker Jack Ham. "For me, every team's goal is to get to the championship, so in some ways this game would be more important than the Super Bowl. This is the game we'd been pointing to since the first day of training camp."

You certainly would've thought the Steelers had been preparing for that game for the previous five months. Pittsburgh looked as prepared and motivated for this game as they had in any of their other playoff contests.

After a typical 3–3 Pittsburgh-Oakland grudge match during the first half, Oakland scored with relative ease in the third quarter, taking a 10–3 lead. The Steelers responded early in the fourth quarter with a nine-play, 61-yard touchdown drive that tied the game.

On their ensuing possession, Ham intercepted a Stabler pass on Oakland's side of the field and returned it to the 9-yard line. Then Terry Bradshaw hit Lynn Swann with a touchdown pass that sealed the game. Pittsburgh had every ounce of momentum. The Raiders didn't have a chance.

One of the most telling statistics from the game is the discrepancy in rushing yards. The Steelers finished with 224, mostly from Franco Harris's 111 and Rocky Bleier's 98, compared to Oakland's 29.

"They beat our butts," Madden conceded after the game.

"The dynasty of Super Bowls was born that day," Harris said.

Ben Roethlisberger celebrates his 4-yard, fourth-quarter touchdown run with receiver Hines Ward in the AFC Championship road win against the Denver Broncos on January 22, 2006, that sent the Steelers to Super Bowl XL.

"We felt that now, we're not a good team, we're a great team."

Of course, behind the Steel Curtain defense, the Steelers went out and took care of business, 16–6, in Super Bowl IX against Minnesota. After the Oakland game, there was no way the Vikings were going to win.

"We proved we could beat a very good team and do it under pressure," Andy Russell said of the AFC Championship Game in

THE ROONEY-MARA CONNECTION

Art Rooney and Giants founder Tim Mara were good friends, even before their days as NFL owners. Tim Mara was a bookmaker in New York and Rooney was one of the country's best bettors. The two clicked immediately. In fact, a couple of stories about their horse escapades have become legendary.

As referenced in the feature story about Rooney in this chapter, one such legend says that after both men had a good day at the track, they decided to buy an NFL franchise. The other is that after Rooney had a great day at the track, he was so happy with his "good-luck charm" Mara that he said he was going to name a son after him. Hence, the naming of Tim Rooney, Art's third son.

A 1937 *Time* article, which compared Rooney's build to that of a football, was titled "Lucky Rooney." It detailed some of Rooney's better days at the track. During a few-day stretch in either 1936 or '37 (depending on the source), Rooney won anywhere from $200,000 to $358,000 (again, depending on the source). He concealed the exact amount he won at Empire City and Saratoga, but legend has it he had to hire an armored truck to take his winnings from New York back home to Pittsburgh.

According to another 1937 article, Mara said, "Rooney started his streak at the Empire Track [in New York]. He won himself $25,000. I told him, 'Stick that dough in your kick and forget about the horses. I ought to know. I'm a bookmaker. It's my business to take money from guys like you.'

"Well, the very next day the horses are running at Saratoga, and I see Rooney. He gets me to mark his [racing] card for him. I said, 'All right, sucker. Go ahead and blow your dough. I'll be here when the races are over if you want car fare back home.'

"Rooney wasn't [placing his bets with] me. He was betting some of the other fellows.... When the races were over, I asked him how he made out. 'Pretty well,' he said. 'I won $108,600. How'd you do?' I didn't tell him, but I'd lost close to three grand on the day."

Regardless of the stories, when they did start their franchises—Mara and the Giants in 1925, then Rooney with the Steelers in 1933—the Rooney and Mara families quickly became synonymous with the NFL and the concept of ideal owners.

John "Frenchy" Fuqua, who's best known for his role in the "Immaculate Reception," played for both Art Rooney and Tim Mara's son, Wellington. Before the 1970 season, the Giants traded Fuqua to the Steelers.

"They were probably two of the most impressive and loving and God-fearing men on this planet," Fuqua said of Rooney and Mara. "Mr. Rooney was just a quiet guy with a cigar, but when he spoke to you it was like a word from the wise. He never said anything bad to you, and even when no one in that locker room would speak to you after a bad game the Chief would come up and say something nice and that would make you want to try that much harder the next Sunday."

Although Art Rooney and Tim Mara are deceased, the Rooney-Mara football connection is as strong today as ever. Tim Mara's grandson, Chris, is married to the Chief's granddaughter, Kathleen, Tim Rooney's daughter. One of Chris and Kathleen's children, daughter Kate, is an actress. Among Kate's roles was the character Annie Cantrell in the 2006 football movie *We Are Marshall*.

Oakland. "After all, the world championship was on the line. We had lost the year before to the Raiders. We beat them in the 'Immaculate Reception' game, but then lost to the Dolphins.

"So to win that game against Oakland in Oakland was incredible. We didn't blow them out; we survived it. But that was the most important game of all time for the Pittsburgh Steelers."

2005: ROAD SWEET ROAD

It stands as one of the most unlikely and remarkable playoff runs in NFL history. So many facets of it are hard to believe. The play of Ben Roethlisberger. The three road wins. Shoot, just the fact that they were even in the playoffs.

Frankly, even as late as December, if someone would've offered you even money on the Steelers reaching the playoffs, you would've thought twice about it.

With four games remaining, after dropping three straight, the Steelers stood at 7–5. It was a far cry from the previous season, when the team cruised to a 15–1 record only to lose in the AFC Championship Game at home against New England.

Art Rooney Sr. and then-NFL commissioner Bert Bell go over draft lists on December 18, 1947.

But suddenly second-year quarterback Roethlisberger took charge of the team. He led the Steelers to convincing wins in their last four games, including a 41–0 dismantling of Cleveland on the road.

The Steelers and their 11–5 record received the sixth seed in the AFC playoffs.

Incidentally, there is a certain coincidence to that three-game losing streak. After dropping the first one at Baltimore, the Steelers went on to lose at Indianapolis and then against Cincinnati. The first two playoff opponents? Cincinnati and Indianapolis.

At Number Three Cincinnati, January 8

The Steelers and Bengals split their games, with each team winning on its opponent's home field, during the regular season. The Bengals finished 11–5 also, but they won the AFC North title by way of a tie-breaker with Pittsburgh.

The teams' trend of winning on each other's home field would continue during their AFC wild-card playoff game. This time, though, the game was decided long before the eventual 31–17 final score.

In the first quarter, on Cincinnati's first pass play of the game, Pro Bowl quarterback Carson Palmer and receiver Chris Henry connected on the longest pass play in Bengal playoff history, 66 yards to the Pittsburgh 22. The cheering didn't last long. Just as Palmer released the ball, Steelers nose tackle Kimo von Oelhoffen, who spent the first six years of his career in Cincinnati, fell into Palmer's knee. Torn anterior cruciate ligament.

"I knew right away that it was bad," Palmer said after the game. "I felt my whole knee pop."

"It was very unfortunate," said von Oelhoffen, who was noticeably upset after the game. "I have a lot of respect for the kid. I wish it didn't happen."

The Bengals had to turn to veteran backup Jon Kitna. Pittsburgh's defense harassed Kitna like their kid brother for the rest of the game, sacking him four times and forcing him to throw two interceptions.

Early in the game, it didn't matter much. The Bengals took a 10–0 lead in the first quarter and still led 17–14 at halftime.

Pittsburgh took control in the third quarter. After Jerome Bettis scored on a five-yard run, giving the Steelers their first lead of the game, the defense stopped Kitna and the Bengals.

On the ensuing possession, the Steelers had the ball on the Cincinnati 43 on third-and-3. Pittsburgh took advantage of shell-shocked Cincinnati by sealing the game with a flea flicker. Receiver Antwaan Randle El lined up next to Roethlisberger in the shotgun, took the snap directly, ran to the right, and tossed the ball over to "Big Ben." Roethlisberger threw to a wide-open Cedric Wilson, who ran it in for the touchdown.

STEELERS ALL-TIME TEAM

As part of the team's 75th anniversary in 2007, the Steelers unveiled the 33 players who earned a spot on the all-time team. The following players were selected by the fans through several outlets in Pittsburgh and on the team's website, www.steelers.com.

Offense

Terry Bradshaw, Quarterback, 1970–83*

Jerome Bettis, Running Back, 1996–2005

Rocky Bleier, Running Back, 1968, 1970–80

Franco Harris, Running Back, 1972–83*

Bennie Cunningham, Tight End, 1976–85

Elbie Nickel, Tight End, 1947–57

John Stallworth, Wide Receiver, 1974–87*

Lynn Swann, Wide Receiver, 1974–82*

Hines Ward, Wide Receiver, 1998–2007**

Larry Brown, Offensive Tackle, 1971–84

Dermontti Dawson, Center, 1988–2000

Alan Faneca, Guard, 1998–2007**

Tunch Ilkin, Offensive Tackle, 1980–92

Jon Kolb, Offensive Tackle, 1969–81

Mike Webster, Center, 1974–88*

Defense

Joe Greene, Defensive Tackle, 1969–81*

L.C. Greenwood, Defensive End, 1969–81

Casey Hampton, Nose Tackle, 2001–07**

Ernie Stautner, Defensive Tackle, 1950–63*

Dwight White, Defensive End, 1971–80

Jack Ham, Outside Linebacker, 1971–82*

Jack Lambert, Middle Linebacker, 1974–84*

Greg Lloyd, Outside Linebacker, 1988–97

Joey Porter, Outside Linebacker, 1999–2006

Andy Russell, Outside Linebacker, 1963, 1966–76

Mel Blount, Cornerback, 1970–83*

Jack Butler, Defensive Back, 1951–59
Carnell Lake, Safety, 1989–98
Troy Polamalu, Safety, 2003–07**
Donnie Shell, Safety, 1974–87
Rod Woodson, Cornerback, 1987–96
Specialists
Gary Anderson, Kicker, 1982–94
Bobby Walden, Punter, 1968–77
* Member of the Pro Football Hall of Fame.
** Active player during the 2007 season.

"We've had that play in there for a while," coach Bill Cowher said. "[Offensive coordinator Ken] Whisenhunt made a great call. It was the perfect situation for it."

Trickery aside, offensively the Steelers were efficient. Three main runners combined for 136 of the team's 144 rushing yards, led by Bettis's 52 yards on 10 carries.

And Roethlisberger, who threw for an unbelievable 386 yards— which was good for third on the team's all-time list at the time—in the loss against the Bengals on December 4, had a solid (albeit slightly tamer) performance this time out. He completed 14 of 19 passes for 208 yards, three touchdowns, and zero interceptions.

"Last year, everything was new to Ben," said wide receiver Hines Ward, who caught one of Roethlisberger's touchdown tosses. "The intangibles that he brings, I like a lot."

A couple of those intangibles would show up the next week against the Colts.

At Number One Indianapolis, January 15

Super Bowl-winning teams aren't always the best team on the field. Sometimes they're lucky. That was the case for the Steelers in getting past the Indianapolis Colts.

For the most part, the Steelers dominated the game, leading by 18 points in the third quarter, 21–3. It turned out to be much closer than that.

As Ed Bouchette best summed up about the Steelers in his

STEELERS LEGENDS TEAM

As part of the team's 75th anniversary in 2007, an eight-member panel selected the 24 Steelers who make up the Steelers Legends Team. These players were an important part of the team's success prior to the 1970 merger with the NFL. These players were eligible for selection on the organization's 75th anniversary all-time team.

Offense

Bobby Layne, Quarterback, 1958–62*

Dick Hoak, Running Back, 1961–70

John Henry Johnson, Running Back, 1960–65*

Elbie Nickel, Tight End, 1947–57

Roy Jefferson, Wide Receiver, 1965–69

Ray Mathews, Wide Receiver, 1951–59

Chuck Cherundolo, Center, 1941–42, 1945–48

Mike Sandusky, Offensive Guard, 1957–65

Bruce Van Dyke, Offensive Guard, 1967–73

Charley Bradshaw, Offensive Tackle, 1961–66

Frank Varrichione, Offensive Tackle, 1955–60

Defense

Gene "Big Daddy" Lipscomb, Defensive Line, 1961–62

Ben McGee, Defensive Line, 1964–72

Bill McPeak, Defensive Line, 1949–57

Ernie Stautner, Defensive Line, 1950–63*

Dale Dodrill, Linebacker, 1951–59

Myron Pottios, Linebacker, 1961–65

Jerry Shipkey, Linebacker, 1948–52

Jack Butler, Defensive Back, 1951–59

Bill Dudley, Defensive Back/Running Back, 1942, 1945–46*

Howard Hartley, Defensive Back, 1949–52

Clendon Thomas, Defensive Back, 1962–68

Specialists

Armand Niccolai, Kicker, 1934–42

Pat Brady, Punter, 1952–54

* Member of the Pro Football Hall of Fame.

game story for the *Pittsburgh Post-Gazette*, "They survived the Indianapolis Colts, 21–18, because quarterback Ben Roethlisberger made a game-saving tackle and the Colts' Mike Vanderjagt, the most accurate field-goal kicker in NFL history, missed badly from 46 yards with 17 seconds left."

After the Colts scored 15 unanswered points in the fourth quarter, they turned the ball over to the Steelers on downs when quarterback Peyton Manning went down at the Indy 2-yard line with 1:33 left in the game.

With a backfield that featured the ever-dependable Bettis, who hadn't fumbled all season, Pittsburgh was in a perfect position to seal the game.

Bettis was headed over to the right side when Indianapolis linebacker Gary Brackett knocked the ball loose. Colts defensive back Nick Harper scooped up the ball and headed toward his end zone. Only one person stood in his way: Roethlisberger.

Roethlisberger got back and, as Harper started to cut to the inside, "Big Ben" barely grabbed Harper around the bottom of his leg and saved the touchdown at the Indianapolis 42.

"Once in a blue moon, Jerome fumbles," Roethlisberger said. "Once in a blue moon, I make a tackle. They just happened to be in the same game."

Still, with a minute remaining, Manning had plenty of time to put his team in a position to score. And he did.

The Colts got down to the 28. Manning took two shots to the end zone to one of his favorite targets, Reggie Wayne. Both passes were broken up by Steelers rookie Bryant McFadden. So Indianapolis head coach Tony Dungy, a former Steelers player and assistant coach, called for Vanderjagt.

The 46-yard field-goal attempt wasn't even close. The Steelers survived, becoming the first number six seed to beat the top seed.

"For us to come in and do what we did today, it took a supreme effort from all three phases of our game," Cowher said. "It was a heck of a football game. There was a lot of ebb and flow in the second half and we weathered it. It was an unbelievable ending."

With the win, the Steelers avenged their 26–7 loss from earlier in the season. The win also put them in the AFC Championship Game.

At Number Two Denver, January 22

After beating the AFC's best team the week before, facing Denver seemed somewhat anticlimactic, and it showed.

The Steelers jumped on the Broncos quickly and often. Pittsburgh scored on each of its first four possessions and took an impressive 24–3 lead on three second-quarter touchdowns: a 12-yard pass play from Roethlisberger to Cedrick Wilson, a 3-yard run by Bettis, and a 17-yard pass from Roethlisberger to Hines Ward.

It didn't hurt the Steelers that Denver quarterback Jake Plummer, who had been relatively good during the year, reverted to ways that his opponents have loved over the years (and Denver fans have loathed). "The Snake" lost two fumbles, threw two interceptions, and was sacked three times—including two by weak-side linebacker Joey Porter—under the pressure of a relentless defense.

In the fourth quarter, the Broncos cut the lead to 27–17, but the Steelers never were threatened.

In winning games at Cincinnati, Indianapolis, and Denver, Pittsburgh became the first-ever number six seed to advance to the Super Bowl. They were just the second team in NFL history to win three road playoff games before reaching the Super Bowl. In that the Steelers joined the 1985 New England Patriots.

"The toughest route they said to take was the scenic route, and that ended up being the best route for us," Porter said. "We went to three different cities and shocked the world three different times. We weren't supposed to be in this situation, but we pulled it off. We pulled it off everywhere we went."

Of course, Pittsburgh's hot streak continued against Seattle in Detroit in Super Bowl XL. But you'll read more about that later in the book.

THE BAD

NOW *THAT* WAS THE PITTS

When Steelers' fans think back to bad Pittsburgh teams trying to come up with the worst, some might want to say 1988, when the team went 5–11 and missed out on the playoffs for the fourth consecutive year. Some older fans might throw in one of the teams from the 1960s, including Chuck Noll's first year, 1969, when the team won its first game before losing every other one that season. Some, through stories they've heard, might mention the infamous "Steagles" of 1943.

Shoot, compared to one team, all of those were champions: the squad known sadly, if not affectionately, as "Card-Pitts."

During the 1940s, professional sports weren't affected any differently than other professions when it came to World War II. Nearly every type of business suffered because many men were fighting overseas. The Cleveland Rams, for instance, lost so many players that they were allowed to suspend play in 1943. That was the same year that the Steelers and the Philadelphia Eagles combined to form the Steagles.

Although the team wasn't good by most standards, it finished with a respectable 5–4–1 record. It's a wonder they won at all considering that Pittsburgh's Walt Kiesling and Philadelphia's Greasy Neale, who shared the head coaching responsibilities, couldn't stand each other.

At the end of the '43 season, the Steagles dissolved automatically based on their agreement with the NFL.

TRIVIA

Since 1951, in how many years have the Steelers failed to have a Pro Bowl player?

Find the answers on pages 165–166.

There was a chance of teaming up again in '44, but the two teams' owners, the Steelers' Art Rooney and Bert Bell, and the Eagles' Lex Thompson, didn't exactly agree on everything either. Both teams' owners wanted what they thought was best for their respective city. When they couldn't agree on the number of "home" games that would be played or where the Steagles' home office would be, Rooney pulled out and went looking for a new team with which the Steelers could merge.

Evidently, the Chicago Cardinals were about the only option, and they weren't exactly a football powerhouse. Saying you wanted to partner with the Cardinals would be like picking a guy on stilts to race Sidney Crosby around a rink.

As *Pittsburgh Press* sports editor Chester Smith wrote of the Cardinals, "The Cards were 0 and 10 last year, and they had a punter, who, while practicing his punts, actually missed the ball. His knee went crashing into his forehead, and he was out for the rest of the season with a fractured skull."

The Card-Pitts had a few of those types. Besides a couple high school players, the roster also included players who received 4-F military classifications (meaning they were physically or mentally unfit to fight) and medically discharged veterans.

Kiesling got along more with his new co-coach, Phil Handler. The two shared a strong penchant for horse racing. Rooney once quipped that Kies "carried *Racing Form* more than the playbook." The combination of hapless players and gambling coaches didn't pay off.

Pardon the expression, but the Card-Pitts were the pits. The team was so bad that after its third game of the year, someone wrote a letter to the *Pittsburgh Post-Gazette* suggesting that the team be called the "Carpits," because "every team in the league walks over them."

The Card-Pitts didn't lose a game by fewer than 14 points after the opener, a two-point loss to Cleveland, and they led their

BY THE NUMBERS

The union between the Steelers and the Chicago Cardinals in 1944, made necessary by World War II, produced the worst squad in the organization's history.

10—The number of games played in 1944.
9—The number of games lost by at least 14 points.
2—The number of head coaches; duties were shared by Chicago's Phil Handler and Pittsburgh's Walt Kiesling.
1—The number of games the team lost by fewer than three points.
0—The total number of wins in 1944.

opponents only three times all season.

Two of those three times came in the Cleveland game. After surrendering a 21–16 lead in the fourth quarter, the Card-Pitts took a 28–23 lead when quarterback Coley McDonough hooked up with Johnny Butler for a 67-yard touchdown reception. It was one of the team's shining moments that season.

The only other bright spot was the play of second-year running back John Grigas, who had played his rookie season with Chicago.

Grigas battled much of the season with New York's Bill Paschal for rushing supremacy in the NFL. After a winless rookie season with the Chicago Cardinals and a winless sophomore campaign, Grigas decided enough was more than plenty.

Before the season finale against the Chicago Bears, Grigas, who was second in the NFL with 610 yards, quit the team. Why stick around for the final game? Although he had told a couple teammates early in the week that he might quit, he bolted in the middle of the night before the Bears game, leaving a note for his roommate Don Currivan and another for the owners. (He played the final three years of his career, 1945–47, with the Boston Yanks.)

The Bears handed Card-Pitts its worst defeat of the year, 49–7.

"The season couldn't have turned out any worse than this one," said co-owner Bert Bell.

Rooney's take wasn't much kinder. "Merging the two teams didn't make us twice as good," he said. "It made us twice as bad!"

SOS: SAME OLD STEELERS

Pardon Steelers founder Art Rooney for the expression. He really didn't realize what he was starting. But there he was, talking with a reporter after the Steelers got new uniforms in the late 1940s. The reporter asked Rooney what he thought about the new look. The Chief surveyed the players running around the field in their new duds and proclaimed, "The only thing different is the uniforms. Inside, it's the same old Steelers."

And a term to describe the losing Steelers was born.

Rooney was right, though. As the old joke goes, there weren't a lot of good things coming out of Pittsburgh during the football season except steel and Interstate 279.

The Steelers, through much of their first 30-some-odd years, were a footnote to sports in Pittsburgh. Rooney traditionally lost money with the team. And sports fans in the city had diversions. Pitt football had some good seasons throughout the 1950s and '60s. And Pittsburgh had its world championship in baseball in 1960, when Bill Mazeroski hit his walk-off homer that beat the Yankees in the World Series. Even though the Pirates struggled throughout much of the '60s, the team remained fun to watch with guys like Roberto Clemente, Willie Stargell, Vern Law, and Bob Veale.

But then there were the Steelers, Pittsburgh's "other" pro team. A team that wasn't as much fun to watch.

In fact, beginning with their inaugural season, 1933, the first time the Steelers had more than two consecutive seasons with a winning record was their first trip to the Super Bowl, following the 1974 season. Before that, the only times they even had back-to-back winning seasons was 1942 and '43, 1958 and '59, and 1962 and '63.

Basically, the team wasn't a complete failure; it just wasn't a champion. As much as anything, the Steelers were unlucky. They had to have been. At least in those winning seasons. After all, they featured men who were larger than life in football at the time: "Bullet" Bill Dudley, Johnny "Blood" McNally, future Supreme

TRIVIA

What former Steeler holds the NCAA record for the longest punt?

Find the answers on pages 165–166.

Court Justice Byron "Whizzer" White, Ernie Stautner, Bobby Layne, and John Henry Johnson. The Steelers teams with these legends played hard on the field. Opponents often commented about being banged up whenever playing the Steelers.

"We finally got so we didn't give a damn for anybody," Stautner said. "We didn't have the material, but we knew that somebody was gonna pay."

"The tradition of the Steelers is hard rock-'em, sock-'em football," added Stautner, who went on to a long post-playing career as an assistant coach for the Dallas Cowboys. "[The Steelers are] proud of that. I was proud of that when I played for the Steelers."

The Steelers were so inept, at least offensively, that during two seasons, 1952 and '57, the team's leading rusher failed to score a single touchdown (Ray Mathews in '52 and Billy Wells in '57). A large part of the problem was that the coaches never had time—or took time—to develop an offensive strategy. Going through 13 head coaches during the team's first 37 years, and tweaking the offense and personnel each time, isn't a blueprint for success.

Since Chuck Noll's arrival in 1969, in 39 seasons the Steelers have had three head coaches. As telling is that before Chuck Noll arrived in 1969, Raymond "Buddy" Parker was the only coach who lasted (or stuck around) more than four seasons. He coached the team from 1957–64. Although he won more than any other coach up to that point, Parker couldn't stand rookies. So he'd trade draft picks and young players for older (translated often as "over the hill") veterans. In 1961 he traded four of the team's first seven picks. (Granted, they still drafted linebacker Myron Pottios and running back Dick Hoak that season.)

Shoot, that's nothing compared to what Parker tried another time.

"On a plane ride home, he would walk back in the aisle of the plane and ask a player to get up so he could sit next to a guy who may have fumbled or dropped a pass. He'd sit there and call him every name in the book," said Hoak, who became a Steeler fixture as an assistant coach after his playing career. "One time, we lost a preseason game, and he put the whole team on waivers. The commissioner's office called the next day and said he couldn't do that. He told them 'Why not? They all stink.' He would just lose it."

Too bad partying didn't translate to wins. Off the field, the Steelers always had a blast. They were hard-drinking, hard-living types who fit in well with the blue-collar town they represented. Besides the normal carousing, there are stories such as how Ray Mathews tried to ride horseback from Pittsburgh to the training camp in Olean, New York. And how McNally simply forgot about games every now and then because he was having too much fun.

Breaking the SOS mold pretty much came out of the blue with the hiring of Noll. Before he arrived, things looked just as bleak as ever.

"We had some good teams in the early 1960s, but in the late '60s we were awful," said Andy Russell, whom the Steelers drafted in 1963. He played with the team that season and then went to Germany for two years with the Army to fulfill his ROTC duty from college. "When I came back in '66, the Steelers weren't the same team. They had been devastated by age. We struggled. We were just awful."

Until the 1970s, not only were the Steelers counted on to lose, but they also became a predictable sort at the start of games. With Walt Kiesling coaching during the mid-1950s, the Steelers had a fullback named Fran Rogel. For whatever reason, on the first offensive play of every game, Kiesling sent Rogel up the middle. It became so obvious that the fans started chanting, "Hey, diddle, diddle, Rogel up the middle." Art Rooney tried to change that. Before one game he told Kiesling that he wanted the Steelers to start off with a pass. That was an order. No exceptions. Pittsburgh did just that. And what a beauty. Steeler quarterback Jack Scarbath faked a handoff to Rogel and then hit Jack McClairen with a pass and McClairen ran it 80 yards for a touchdown! Only thing was, a Steeler lineman was offside. Oh well, good try. "I found out later," Rooney said, "that Kies had ordered that lineman to go offside. Kies told the players, 'If this pass play works, that Rooney will be down here every week giving us plays.' Gentlemen, that was the first and last time I ever tried to send in a play."

Of course, on their next play, Rogel ran up the middle. Good for one yard.

That story pretty much sums up the "Same Old Steelers."

It took a while for things to get better, even with Chuck Noll taking over as the head coach in 1969 and the talented group of players they started drafting that year, beginning with Joe Greene. It didn't matter at first. Pittsburgh wasn't an easy sell.

As Dwight White, whom the Steelers drafted in 1971 out of East Texas State, says, "I was in Los Angeles with my agent for the NFL draft. I got the call I had been waiting for…almost. 'Dwight, this is Chuck Noll from Pittsburgh. I want to let you know we just drafted you in the fourth round. We think there's a lot of opportunity here in Pittsburgh.' When I hung up the phone, in all the excitement, I couldn't remember if he said Pittsburgh or Philadelphia. Then I realized, 'Pittsburgh, Pittsburgh? I've got to go to Pittsburgh?' Pittsburgh at that point was in the bowels of the NFL.

"I thought life was as dark as it could get, being drafted by the Pittsburgh Steelers."

The decade of the 1960s ended, appropriately, with the Steelers finishing with one of their worst seasons ever. It certainly was their most discouraging because they started off with a win, which gave them the feeling that the "Same Old Steelers" moniker was vanishing. But then they reeled off 13 consecutive losses.

"Sometimes it gets discouraging," Greene said late in the 1969 season, "but we always have the next game to look forward to. We feel like Pittsburgh is a team of the future. This is not a dead Steeler team like I've always read about.

"There's plenty of life here, and we think all the time that the next game will be the one to start us off. We'll put it all together before too long. Then we'll see. We've come close to whipping a lot of folks. We're just missing by a little."

They wouldn't miss for much longer.

LIVING UP TO A "MEAN" NICKNAME

Without question, "Mean" Joe Greene was the cog for the Steelers defensive dominance during the 1970s. And even though each team in the league had its "enforcer," here are some of the bad and ugly times when Greene lived up to his nickname.

October 12, 1969 Greene, during his fourth regular-season NFL game, leveled New York Giants quarterback Fran Tarkenton with a late hit. Greene was ejected from the game. The Steelers lost 10–7.

November 23, 1969 Greene punched Minnesota Vikings guard Jim Vellone. It was one play after Greene gave Vellone a forearm shiver. The Steelers were penalized 30 yards. Greene got the boot. The Steelers lost 52–14.

October 5, 1975 Greene, using his most infamous fighting technique of kicking an opponent when he was down, was ejected from the game against Cleveland for continually kicking Browns' guard Bob McKay in the groin. There was another game against the Browns when Cleveland center Bob DeMarco gave Greene an elbow to the throat. No penalty was called. So Greene ran over toward the Cleveland bench and clotheslined DeMarco. "I think he lost some teeth," Greene said in 2000.

December 24, 1977 Greene wasn't feeling very jolly during this Christmas Eve AFC playoff game at Denver. Greene punched Bronco lineman Paul Howard with a right to the stomach. Even though Howard had to be helped off the field, the officials didn't see it. On the next play, Greene punched Denver center Mike Montler. The officials saw that one and ejected Greene from the game. The Steelers lost 34–21.

THE MEAN SIDE OF JOE

Although "Mean" Joe Greene's tenacity on the field was an example for other players on the Steel Curtain and around the league, that wasn't always the case. Greene's rookie year of 1969, playing on a team that ended up losing 13 consecutive games, was his most frustrating. Greene found himself getting kicked out of a few games that year.

One of the most memorable came late in the season when the

Joe Greene (75) plows into an unidentified Eagles running back during a September 1969 game in Philadelphia.

Steelers took a 1–8 record to Minnesota. Greene, who hated losing and wasn't taking to the idea well, was getting frustrated. During the game, Greene and Vikings guard Jim Vellone were going at it. Finally, when Vellone hit Greene from behind, Greene took a forearm to Vellone. A flag was thrown.

"I was sure it was on him," Greene said after the game. "But come to find out, it was on me. I got kind of hot about it. I just can't stand being pushed around. So I said, 'No. 63 [Vellone], I'm gonna getcha.'"

And he did, with another forearm. Greene was ejected.

At that time, since many NFL teams used baseball stadiums as their home turf, usually the best way to set it up was to have both sidelines on the same side of the field. Although it was really the

DID YOU KNOW...

The Steelers drafted Gene Keady in the 19th round of the 1958 draft? Keady, who was a standout receiver and defensive back at Kansas State, injured a knee four weeks into training camp in '58. Coach Buddy Parker suggested Keady return in 1959 to try out as a defensive back. It never happened. Needing a job, Keady became the head basketball coach, head golf coach, and a teacher at Beloit (Kansas) High School. After various assistant coaching positions at the college level, Keady eventually became a household name in basketball circles as the longtime head coach at Purdue.

only way to lay it out, having fierce competitors with idle time just a few feet from each other was less than ideal.

As Greene walked toward the Pittsburgh bench after getting tossed, Minnesota veterans Carl Eller and Alan Page started giving him a hard time.

"They were saying things like 'Hey, rookie, you better shape up,'" linebacker Andy Russell remembered. "He didn't look at them, but he was already furious. He went over to the tool box at our bench, grabbed a pair of scissors, and with a madness in his eyes he ran at [Eller and Page] like he was going to slash them. They ran up into the stands. It was a classic bluff; I'm sure he wouldn't have done anything, but they thought he was nuts."

But Greene had earned Vellone's respect—or maybe he wasn't a fan of scissors. Regardless, after the game, with All-Pro Page nearby, Vellone said, "I'll take a punch from a guy as good as Greene anytime. I always thought Alan Page was the best rookie tackle I ever saw, but Greene can do things that Page couldn't do."

Greene continued to take his aggression out on opposing players. Even footballs and helmets weren't safe from Greene's wrath. There was the time he took his helmet and smashed it on a goal post. And then there was the game at Philadelphia early in his career when the Eagles had just made a first down. Greene was enraged because he felt the Eagles were getting away with holding penalties.

"He took the ball away from the refs and he said this game's over," Russell said. "There were about 10 minutes left. Then he threw the ball behind our bench. The officials didn't know what to do. They came over to me and said, 'Captain Russell, would you talk to Mr. Greene?' I said, 'I'm not talking to him.' Were they crazy? So they brought another ball out, thinking that was the solution. Joe took that ball and threw it up in the upper tiers of the stadium. [Terry] Bradshaw couldn't have thrown it as far as Joe did."

With the losing atmosphere the Steelers developed during the 1960s, Greene was simply frustrated. He was bringing not only a toughness that mirrored the perception of the city's steel heritage and a toughness that the organization had never seen, but he was also bringing a winning attitude that the organization hadn't experienced in years. He expected to be on the winning side every time he took the field.

"Losing was not something that I tolerated," Greene said. "Coming to Pittsburgh, I didn't want to tolerate it. It was as simple as that. That was the reason for all my tirades and outbursts."

Over time, Greene controlled his temper. Usually. But he remained one of the game's most dominating players on either side of the football.

1994: THREE YARDS SHY

The discrepancy was impressive: 415 yards to 226. The 10-point lead in the third quarter, at home, seemed to be enough. Especially with the way quarterback Neil O'Donnell was throwing, with AFC title game records of 32-for-54 passing and a Steelers' postseason record 349 yards. Also, he didn't throw any interceptions and he wasn't sacked.

"You could throw for 550 yards and it doesn't matter unless you win," O'Donnell said after the game.

Oh, yeah. There was one slight issue with those numbers. The Steelers somehow snatched defeat from the jaws of victory against San Diego in the 1994 AFC Championship Game at a rainy Three Rivers Stadium. The 17–13 final sent the Chargers to the Super

Bowl and left the Steelers to wonder what happened.

"Had we been shut out," Steelers offensive coordinator Ron Erhardt said afterward, "or nothing happened on offense, you'd say you don't deserve it. But when you dominate a team the way we did offensively, it's discouraging; it's disgusting not to be in the big one."

That's not to say the Steelers didn't have a good defense. In fact, the "Blitzburgh" defense finished second overall in the NFL, just 13 yards behind Dallas. They led the NFL with 55 sacks, including Kevin Greene's 14, which ranks in a tie for second of all time for the Steelers, and Greg Lloyd's 10. The 55 sacks are tied with the 2001 unit for the most in team history. They also allowed only 19 touchdowns—good for first in the NFL in 1994—during the season.

Against the Chargers, though, the Steelers had two uncharacteristic defensive lapses that proved costly, giving the Chargers 14 points.

The first came two minutes after Gary Anderson's 23-yard field goal gave Pittsburgh a 13–3 lead with 10 minutes, 37 seconds left in the third quarter.

With the ball at Pittsburgh's 43, San Diego quarterback Stan Humphries faked a handoff to his big runner Natrone Means and then hit a streaking tight end, Alfred Pupunu, who had gotten past cornerback Deon Figures and safety Carnell Lake, both of whom went for the fake to Means. Pupunu caught the ball at the 20 and ran the rest of the way for the score.

The other decisive play came in the game's final few minutes. On third-and-14, Humphries and receiver Tony Martin burned another Pittsburgh cornerback, Tim McKyer, for a 43-yard touchdown play that gave San Diego a 17–13 lead with 5:13 left.

Throughout the game, the Chargers looked like a team on a mission. They weren't about to roll over for the vaunted Steelers. There's a reason besides the Super Bowl. The Steelers gave the underdog Chargers some bulletin board material by planning a Super Bowl rap video—before the AFC title game.

"I wonder what these guys are going to do with their Super Bowl video now," San Diego safety Stanley Richard said after the game. "Maybe we need to get their coordinator over to San Diego so we can get our own video going."

"We were close and we felt good," Levon Kirkland, who led the Steelers with 10 tackles against the Chargers, said years later of the video. "But honestly we hadn't done anything at that point. I'm in the [video] meeting thinking: this is not good. We were already planning for something that we hadn't done yet."

Defensive lapses and premature Super Bowl videos aside, the Steelers had one final chance to win the game. They had the ball at San Diego's 3-yard line on fourth down with a little more than a minute left in the fourth quarter. The game ended, in essence, when O'Donnell threw a low pass to Barry Foster in the middle of the end zone. San Diego linebacker Dennis Gibson deflected the ball.

Just three yards shy.

RENEWING A RIVALRY IN THE PROMISED LAND

Some facts need to be set right off the bat about Neil O'Donnell, the Steelers' third-round draft pick in 1990. During his time with the Steelers, 1990–95, O'Donnell was a dependable quarterback. He ranks third on the team's all-time passing list with 12,867 yards. He's tied for first, with Tommy Maddox, for most 300-yard games in a season (4). He's second of all time on the team with a passer rating of 81.6. He's third on the team with a 57.1 percent career completion percentage. And he's not listed among the career or season leaders with passes intercepted.

In 1992, his second year in the league, O'Donnell received his first and only Pro Bowl selection. Which brings us to 1995, Super Bowl XXX, and O'Donnell's performance, which should receive a rating of XXX.

As with any Super Bowl season, there were certain hiccups along the way in 1995 that wouldn't have made a strong case for the Steelers as the AFC's representative in the league's marquee game. The Steelers won their first two games but then went on a quick slide. They dropped two in a row, won one, and then lost two more in a row. So, after seven games, Pittsburgh's record was a less-than-champion-worthy 3–4.

Even though the Steelers finished the regular season with the

THE PLAYER OF THE '90S

One key to the Steelers' slow start in 1995 was that one of the best Steelers of all time, and possibly *the* best player of the 1990s, Rod Woodson, went down with a knee injury against Detroit in the first game of the year. He went to tackle Barry Sanders and his right knee gave out.

Albeit miraculous that he played at all during the season after the injury, Woodson didn't return until the Super Bowl.

That was a huge blow. After all, since 1987, Woodson had established himself as one of the top defensive and special teams players in the league.

Woodson, who was the NFL's Defensive Player of the Year in 1993, was one of five active players selected for the NFL's 75th Anniversary Team in 1994. Besides his ability as a blazing fast cornerback, Woodson became the organization's best-ever punt returner and kick returner.

"Probably the best athlete I have ever coached," Bill Cowher said of Woodson. "The guy was an unbelievable student of the game. He had a great feel for the game, and you couple that with athletic ability, without a doubt he was the best football player I coached in my fifteen years."

Woodson spent one more season in Pittsburgh before signing with San Francisco. The break-up was messy, with words being exchanged through the media between Woodson and Dan Rooney, but Woodson's teammates didn't hold any grudges.

"Rod is going into the last years of his profession with the best opportunity for him to win a Super Bowl ring," said Steelers safety Carnell Lake. "He will be thrust into a situation in San Francisco where he will play on grass and will have great weather. I see Rod on his way to another Pro Bowl."

Lake should join the Psychic Friends Network. Woodson did all of those things. He played for three teams—San Francisco, Baltimore, and Oakland—for seven more seasons after leaving the Steelers. He led the NFL in interceptions in 1999 and 2000, added four more trips to the Pro Bowl and two more All-Pro selections to his resume.

In 1997, Woodson helped the 49ers reach the NFC Championship Game. Then, in 2000, he won a Super Bowl ring with Baltimore, where he moved from cornerback to safety. He ended his career with the Oakland

Raiders, but not before playing in Super Bowl XXXVII against Tampa Bay.

Woodson is the only player in NFL history to make it to the Pro Bowl in different years as a cornerback, safety, and kick returner.

"I think it's unfair to the rest of the [Raiders players] how many great coaches I've had in my career, especially defensive coaches," Woodson told The New York Times in 2003. "Tony Dungy was my defensive backs coach. Chuck Noll was the head coach. Tony taught me the angles, and the reading and yelling a feel for my footwork, understanding it all. I was uncomfortable for about a year. But like doing anything over time, that green light kicks in and it's, 'Wow, I can do this.'"

And Woodson did. Well done.

second-best record in the AFC at 11–5, no other team in the Central Division had at least a .500 record. Cincinnati and Houston both sported 7–9 records. Indeed, Central was a pushover division that season.

Still, with a win over Buffalo and then a thrilling home win in the AFC Championship Game over Indianapolis, the Steelers were headed to their first Super Bowl since beating the Rams in XIV. The Steelers were headed there on the arm of O'Donnell, who was the NFL's career leader in fewest interceptions per pass attempt.

In the NFC, the best team recordwise, Dallas at 12–4, had little problem in its two playoff games behind a high-powered offense that featured Troy Aikman, Michael Irvin, and Emmitt Smith. The Cowboys crushed Philadelphia 30–11, and then cruised past Green Bay, 38–27, earning its spot in Super Bowl XXX.

One of the great postseason rivalries was being renewed in Tempe, Arizona.

It looked like the Cowboys were going to run away with the game early when they took a 13–0 lead in the second quarter. Right before the half, O'Donnell found Yancey Thigpen for a six-yard touchdown that made the first half look respectable.

O'Donnell changed that thought in the third quarter. Midway through the quarter, the normally accurate O'Donnell was extremely accurate when he hit Larry Brown in the numbers. That would be Larry Brown of the Cowboys—not the Steelers' player who had retired about 10 years earlier.

"The ball just slipped out of my hands," O'Donnell said. "It's something that happens."

Emmitt Smith scored two plays later with a one-yard run, giving Dallas a 20–7 lead midway through the third quarter.

O'Donnell's second interception, the one that turned Brown into a Super Bowl MVP, was the killer, though. The Steelers, trailing 20–10, recovered an onside kick and went down to score a touchdown on a one-yard run by Bam Morris with six minutes, 36 seconds left in the game. On the ensuing possession, Pittsburgh forced Dallas to punt. Suddenly, the Steelers had the ball back with momentum and less than five minutes remaining in the game.

With about four minutes left, O'Donnell threw a perfect pass to Brown. Again. Brown returned it 33 yards, and Smith scored two plays later. On this interception, O'Donnell thought wide receiver Andre Hastings was running an out pattern, while Hastings ran a hitch route.

"It was a bit of miscommunication between quarterback and receiver," O'Donnell said afterward.

Besides the two perfect passes to Brown, O'Donnell looked flustered most of the game. He never seemed to get into a rhythm. He threw a third interception on the game's final play. The Cowboys won the game 27–17.

How bad was O'Donnell's play that game? O'Donnell signed as a free agent with the New York Jets in 1996. He spent two seasons there before going to Cincinnati. In the days leading up to the first meeting between the Steelers and the Bengals in 1998, three years after Super Bowl XXX—*three years later*—Pittsburgh safety Lee Flowers suggested that O'Donnell still needed to apologize to the Steelers for throwing the two ill-advised interceptions to Brown.

"I don't read into any of that stuff," O'Donnell said of Flowers's comments a day later. "I know what happened that game. That's all ancient history right now. I was very upset with the outcome of that game. I think a lot of us were. I put that behind me, though. I've been out of there now for three years, so right now I'm focused on what's at hand, and that's playing for the Bengals."

Of course, during the telephone press conference with reporters, O'Donnell was then asked what did happen in Super Bowl XXX.

"Come on, guys," he said. "Don't let me redo that. That's ancient history."

O'Donnell indeed was focused on the task at hand, proving Super Bowl XXX was ancient history. He torched the Steelers for 298 yards on 20-of-26 passing, three touchdowns, and no interceptions in Cincinnati's last-minute 25–20 win. It was one of only three wins for the Bengals that season. By the way, although two of Cincinnati's three wins came against Pittsburgh that season, O'Donnell faced the Steelers just once.

THE UGLY

THE BIZARRE TALE OF "BIG DADDY" LIPSCOMB

Until the whistle blew, Eugene "Big Daddy" Lipscomb was a menacing defensive tackle. His size of 6'6" and nearly 300 pounds was unheard of at that time in the NFL. Lipscomb easily moved offensive linemen out of his way with a helmet slap and then headed for the opposing quarterback. He was fast and agile enough that he could cover receivers down the field.

There are many stories about how Lipscomb dominated opponents during his 10-year career, which included stops with the Los Angeles Rams (1953–55), the Baltimore Colts (1956–60), and the Steelers (1961–62). There was the time he covered Green Bay's speedy running back Tom Moore for 40 yards and then broke up the pass in the end zone. Or the times when Cleveland would use four men to block him.

But when the whistle blew, the showman in him came out. After using an opponent as a rag doll, Lipscomb would pick up the stunned player, dust him off, and then shoo him toward his huddle. Fans loved it. And Big Daddy, a boisterous and carefree man, adored the attention.

In spite of his abilities on the field, Lipscomb couldn't escape personal tragedy.

A self-proclaimed "B and B man" (booze and broads), Lipscomb handled both as easily, as often, and with as much zeal as he did chasing small quarterbacks. Basically, he loved life no matter what he was doing.

Gene 'Big Daddy' Lipscomb closes in for a sack of Dallas Cowboys quarterback
Eddie LeBaron in 1961.

BY THE NUMBERS

13—The most consecutive losses in the same season, from September 28 to December 21, 1969. The team's lone win that season—Chuck Noll's first as head coach—was in the opener, 16–13 over Detroit.

On the morning of May 10, 1963, however, after a night of mixing the Bs with heroin, "Big Daddy" Lipscomb died of an overdose in Baltimore. He was 31. That much is known to be true. But those are the only hard facts from that night.

Timothy Black, a seedy character who had served time, is the only person who ever offered an eyewitness account of that fateful night. According to Black, he and Lipscomb hooked up late at night on May 9 in Lipscomb's yellow Cadillac. They picked up a couple of seedy ladies and hung out until about 3:00 in the morning. After that, at Lipscomb's urging—according to Black—the two men went out and bought a $12 bag of heroin. They went back to Black's apartment, prepared the heroin, and shot it up.

Lipscomb began to foam at the mouth. Black says he and an acquaintance tried to revive Lipscomb. They called an ambulance. A few hours later, "Big Daddy" Lipscomb died on the way to the hospital.

Lipscomb's friends, family, and former teammates were shocked. They all said how "Big Daddy" hated pain—and especially the pain associated with needles. There was no way he had used heroin before that night. Black would tell investigators that Lipscomb had been using heroin three times a week for six months.

Even Dr. Rudiger Breitenecker, who performed the autopsy, seemed to question Black's account of Lipscomb's usage.

"There is hardly evidence to call him an addict," Breitenecker said. "We cannot, as a matter of fact, say positively that he ever took more than one shot of heroin in his life."

Whether he took 75 shots or just one, it didn't matter. As Edward Linn wrote in *The Saturday Evening Post* on July 27, 1963,

TRIVIA

Who is the only opponent to win at Pittsburgh twice in the same season?

Find the answers on pages 165–166.

"Daddy lived grandly, but he died bad. Which proves again that, one way or another, the world has its ways for grinding down the man of muscle and sweat."

It was a sad end to a hard-lived life. As a child, Lipscomb never knew his father. When Lipscomb was 11 years old, his mother died after being stabbed 47 times by her boyfriend. Lipscomb went to live with his grandparents, who made him get a job so he could pay them rent. After graduating from Detroit's Miller High School, Lipscomb skipped college and enlisted in the Marines.

The Rams noticed him in 1953 on a Marine team at Camp Pendleton in California. That was his first really good bit of fortune.

Lipscomb spent three seasons with the Rams before a five-year stint with the Colts. He helped lead Baltimore to consecutive NFL championships in 1958 and '59, but then the Colts traded Lipscomb to the Steelers in 1961. Lipscomb, who tried his hand at pro wrestling during two off-seasons toward the end of his career, had two good seasons for the Steelers.

Off the field, Lipscomb and Bobby Layne and others routinely enjoyed themselves at various Pittsburgh watering holes, and in Lipscomb's case, with various women. During one stretch, Lipscomb was married to two women. That was nothing.

Steeler defensive back Brady Keys told *Sports Illustrated* writer William Nack about the scene on certain mornings when he'd drive over to Lipscomb's to pick him up.

"There would be three or four women, and they would be half naked," Keys said. "Big Daddy had enough energy for them all. He was always drunk. And he always had cash lying all over the place."

Lipscomb was a three-time Pro Bowl player, including his last season with the Steelers. In two Pro Bowl games, Lipscomb became the game's MVP. In the game after the '62 season, Lipscomb recorded 11 tackles, forced two fumbles, and blocked a pass.

That would be his final game.

Thousands of people, including at least three women who

claimed to be engaged to Big Daddy, went to Charlie Law's funeral home in Baltimore to pay their last respects. To mourn. To gawk. The line stretched two blocks for about 12 hours.

"It was overwhelming," said Baltimore Colts' Hall of Fame running back Lenny Moore. "You'd have thought it was a big movie star in there. Or a head of state. Biggest thing I ever saw like that in this town."

Really, in death as in life, it was just Lipscomb being "Big Daddy."

MIKE WEBSTER: A FALLEN WARRIOR

There's a photograph from 1984 of Mike Webster, the Steelers Hall of Fame center. He resembles a warrior of any time or place, striding triumphantly off the field of battle. He's carrying his helmet. His hair is wet from perspiration. His knuckles and wrists are taped. There are drops of blood below the No. 52 on his white jersey as well as on his gold pants.

For 17 years, 1974–90, Mike Webster gave his sweat, his blood (as well as the blood of others), and really everything he had to the Steelers (1974–88), the Kansas City Chiefs, and the game of football.

Webster was tough. He was a throwback.

"The sight of Mike Webster on a cold, snowy winter day taking the field with short sleeves was the one picture that symbolized the strength and toughness of the Pittsburgh team," former Steelers center Dermontti Dawson said.

Picked by the Steelers in the fifth round of the 1974 draft out of Wisconsin, Webster joined three other future Hall of Famers taken by the team: Lynn Swann, Jack Lambert, and John Stallworth.

Webster backed up Ray Mansfield at center for two years before becoming a starter. He went on to play a team-record 15 seasons with the Steelers and set the model for consistency by playing in 220 games, including 177 consecutive games. That streak might've been longer if it hadn't been for a dislocated elbow that kept him out of four games in 1986.

"I'm not sure I was a Hall of Famer," Webster said during a conference call in January 1997, minutes after the Pro Football Hall of

Mike Webster, the indestructible Steeler with the rolled-up shirt sleeves and a look that warned "don't tread on me," never met another man he couldn't beat on the football field.

Fame's selection committee saw otherwise. "I was there every Sunday, and I did everything I could to be as good as I could be."

Former teammates with the Steelers will point to Webster's play and consistency as one of the cogs in the team's success throughout the 1970s, including Super Bowls XIII and XIV. Then, at the end of Webster's career, the Chiefs signed him hoping that their young guys could learn from his work ethic and dedication to the game.

"I've never seen anybody like Mike Webster. He is the most professional football player I've ever met," quarterback Steve

TRIVIA

What team did the Steelers beat in 2007 that gave them the distinction of beating every team on the road during their 75-year history?

Find the answers on pages 165–166.

DeBerg, who played with Webster in Kansas City, told *The Kansas City Star* in December 1990. "To be honest, I think Mike Webster has had a very big influence on the reasons I'm playing well this year. He was my roommate in training camp. He's my roommate on the road. His professionalism just wears off on you. The guy is amazing. I feel really honored to be exposed to a guy like that. I feel he has had an impact on my performance."

DeBerg, who had been in the league 11 years before taking snaps from Webster, went on to have the third-best season of his career with 3,444 passing yards in 1990.

After spending those last two years with the Chiefs, Webster, like so many ex-athletes, struggled to find a post-playing life. Business deals fell through, costing him his finances. Things were so bad at times that his family couldn't even afford toilet paper. His marriage fell apart and his wife moved with their four kids to her hometown of Lodi, Wisconsin.

All the while, Webster's health was deteriorating. He endured constant pain, headaches.

He was homeless at times, sleeping in his car or at a Pittsburgh train station. Sometimes he'd stay at a budget motel near the Pittsburgh airport. He was a volunteer assistant strength and conditioning coach for about nine months with the Chiefs, and he'd sleep in the equipment room, hoping no one would find out.

"Mike would not accept any assistance for any reason," said Chiefs president and general manager Carl Peterson. "I knew he was having not only financial problems but also health problems, but he would never allow anyone to try to help him. He'd just disappear."

"My problems are my problems," Webster would say.

Those problems mounted. In 1999, Webster was diagnosed finally with brain damage from repeated and long-term head trauma—basically, dementia. Also that year, in September,

Webster pleaded no contest to forging a prescription for Ritalin. He was placed on probation.

The dementia worsened. Webster would forget where he lived. And the damn pain wouldn't go away. His head, his back, his shoulder, his knees, his feet. Seemingly every inch of his body hurt. It would get so bad that Webster stunned himself with a Taser gun in order to sleep.

Throughout the early part of the 21st century, a battle increased between retired NFL players, the NFL, and the NFL Players Association over, mainly, benefits. Diseases and ailments such as dementia, Alzheimers, and numerous back, knee, and hip problems started taking their toll on a large number of players. According to many ex-players, the NFLPA, led by Gene Upshaw, turned its back on its own when they were in desperate need.

Former players receive benefits based on time of service and when the injuries occurred. Although an alarmingly high number of players are suffering from dementia-type illnesses—including former Steeler Ralph Wenzel—the NFL Players Association has argued that there isn't a correlation between head injuries and life as an NFL player.

Webster was convinced to seek benefits. He unintentionally became the poster child for the ex-players' cause.

The NFLPA argued that Webster didn't qualify for full benefits because there was no evidence in their eyes that his problems started before 1996. However, Webster was awarded—and won in an appeal seven years later, in December 2006—full benefits retroactive to his retirement in 1991.

Tragically, he wasn't able to see the fight against the NFLPA to the end. On September 24, 2002, Mike Webster's physical and mental pain went away forever. He died of an apparent heart attack. He was 50.

About two years before Webster died, one of his sons, Garrett, moved to Pittsburgh mainly to be with him, but also to play high school football in Pennsylvania.

"Normally it's the parent waking up the son to go to school," Garrett Webster, then 22, told *The New York Times* in 2006. "With us, it was me waking him up to tell him to take me to school.

DID YOU KNOW...

George Kiick, the father of former NFL running back Jim Kiick, played two seasons for the Steelers, 1940 and '45? Jim Kiick played for the Miami Dolphins during their perfect 17–0 season in 1972.

There were times it did get to be too much for me, but there is no way I would trade what I went through. I loved the moments when we sat in a car and shared a pizza or sat in an apartment with no furniture and watched a movie because we didn't have anything else to do. Those memories made me grow up faster, but I wouldn't trade them for anything."

WHAT WERE THEY THINKING?

Teams in the NFL are just like any other workplace or any other place in society. There are the good, civic-minded people. There are the people who just go about their business every day. And there are those who leave a trail of head-scratchers, people wondering, "What were they thinking?"

Although the Steelers have had their share, four of the stories stand out above the others.

Steve Courson

Steve Courson, an offensive lineman on the Steelers' Super Bowl XIII and XIV teams, had kept silent long enough. He was nearing the end of his career and he was having heart problems, which he was convinced were caused by his steroid use. So, Courson, then playing for Tampa Bay, came clean in 1985. The next year, he was out of football.

In 1991, Courson wrote *False Glory: Steelers and Steroids, The Steve Courson Story*, a tell-all memoir about steroid use through his nine-year career in the NFL.

Courson, who was one of the first NFL players to admit

steroid use, shocked much of Steeler Nation with his revelation. He alleged that head coach Chuck Noll and owner Art Rooney knew that many players were using steroids, which weren't banned at the time.

In the spring of 2005, Courson testified in front of Congress. Six months later, he died. Courson's death, however, was not tied in with his steroid use or heart condition.

Courson was killed on November 10 when a 44 foot-tall tree he was cutting down landed on him. He was 50. Investigators believe Courson was trying to save his dog from the falling tree.

"The wind was blowing, the tree snapped, and it fell on him and his dog," said Roger Victor, an investigator for the Fayette County (Pennsylvania) coroner.

Terry Long

For eight years, 1984–91, Terry Long started at right guard for the Steelers. According to the Associated Press, Long, who was suspended for violating the league's steroid policy, tried to commit suicide with rat poison after that.

In March 2005, Long was charged with burning down Value Added Foods, a poultry-processing plant that he owned, in order to collect the insurance. Since the fire in 2003, Long received $1.19 million from Penn National Insurance Co. for the claim. Also as part of the indictment, Long was charged with fraudulently obtaining about $1.17 million in state loans and grants.

On top of that, while he was in court, Long was told that a warrant had been issued for his arrest in Kansas City for passing a bad check of at least $500.

Long's life was in shambles. His second marriage seemed to be going downhill.

On June 7, Long was found unresponsive at his home. He was rushed to the hospital where he died a few hours later. Originally, the coroner ruled that the 45-year-old Long died of meningitis, which was caused by football-related head trauma. Not so fast.

Four months later, after toxicology reports came back, the cause of Long's death was changed to suicide from drinking antifreeze.

DID YOU KNOW...

Three players appeared in at least 200 games for the Steelers?
Mike Webster, 220 games, 1974–88
Donnie Shell, 201 games, 1974–87
Mel Blount, 200 games, 1970–83
Webster also holds the team record for most seasons (15) and most consecutive games played (177).

Justin Strzelczyk

Justin Strzelczyk was the ideal player, the ideal teammate. During his 10-year career with the Steelers, 1990–99, Strzelczyk played nearly every position on the offensive line. Off the field, he liked to have fun, whether that meant enjoying some adult beverages with friends or hanging out with his young son and daughter.

After his career, Strzelczyk stayed in the Pittsburgh area, where he opened a custom hubcap business.

Strzelczyk admitted to using anabolic steroids for about 10 months during his career. Whether that led to what happened next, no one knows. But on September 30, 2004, Strzelczyk led police on a 40-mile high-speed chase in New York, about 400 miles from his home.

The chase, which reached speeds upwards of 90 miles per hour, ended when Strzelczyk, driving the wrong way for the previous four miles, hit a tanker truck head-on. The fiery crash threw Strzelczyk's body about 80 yards. Somewhat surprisingly, the toxicology report showed no alcohol or drugs in Strzelczyk's system.

"An aunt who was a psychiatric nurse thought he might have been bipolar or manic depressive," said James Hunt, one of the police investigators. "Some people said they could see it coming. We don't think he committed suicide, and if he was truly suffering from a mental illness, he had to believe he was invincible and wouldn't be hurt. Why did it happen? We may never really know."

Richard Seigler

Richard Seigler didn't play much for the Steelers. Although he spent parts of two seasons with the team, his only action came in two games during the 2006 season. But talk about your bad days.

In May 2007, with rumors that the police might be investigating the linebacker, the Steelers released Seigler. That investigation came to a head hours later when police arrested him. Allegedly, Seigler had a little business on the side in Las Vegas. He was, well, a pimp. Seigler was charged with three prostitution-related felonies, including pandering and living off earnings from a prostitute.

ROETHLISBERGER MAKES A BONEHEADED MISTAKE

For all that he has done right during his career thus far with the Steelers, quarterback Ben Roethlisberger nearly lost it all shortly before the 2006 season.

Around 11:30 on the morning of Monday, June 12, Roethlisberger was thrown from his black 2005 Suzuki Hayabusa when a Chrysler New Yorker, traveling in the opposite direction, turned in front of Roethlisberger. The accident occurred in Uptown on Second Avenue near 10th Street. Now, motorcycle accidents happen every day. Probably hundreds, if not thousands, a day. But this one was different. Besides the fact that it happened to the starting quarterback of the defending NFL champs, Roethlisberger wasn't wearing a helmet.

According to reports, Roethlisberger flew headfirst into the windshield of the New Yorker and then landed headfirst on the concrete. He broke his jaw and his nose, and ruptured a major blood vessel in his mouth, which was draining blood into his stomach. He later told ESPN that he was "literally seconds, maybe a minute, away from dying."

Ironically, a story ran in the *Pittsburgh Tribune-Review* on the morning of the accident about Roethlisberger riding his motorcycle and doing so without a helmet. Roethlisberger and Steelers head coach Bill Cowher had met about Roethlisberger's motorcycle that weekend.

"We talked about being a risk taker, and I'm not really a risk taker," Roethlisberger told the paper regarding his meeting with Cowher. "I'm pretty conservative and laid back. So the big thing is just to be careful and that's what we do. I think every person that rides is careful. And that's the biggest thing. I'll just continue to be careful."

In that same article, when asked about wearing a helmet, Roethlisberger said, "I think that's at your own discretion. Obviously, Pennsylvania doesn't think people need to."

At the time, Pennsylvania law stated that riders at least 21 years old, who completed a safety course or had been licensed at least two years, did not have to wear a helmet.

Three days after the accident, Roethlisberger issued a public statement that read, "In the past few days, I have gained a new perspective on life. By the grace of God, I am fortunate to be alive, surrounded by loved ones, and lifted by the prayers and support of so many. I am sorry for any anxiety and concern my actions have caused others, specifically my family, the Steelers organization, my teammates, and our fans.

"I was confident in my ability to ride a motorcycle and simply believed such an accident would not happen to me. If I ever ride again, it certainly will be with a helmet."

Of course, a month later, during a round of interviews for the first time since the accident, Roethlisberger told ABC's *Good Morning America* that on the day of the wreck he was supposed to take his helmet to get it custom painted to match his bike so he could "wear it all the time when I rode that bike. And I totally forgot it that day."

Oops.

What's worse is that Roethlisberger and every other professional athlete got a real-life warning a year earlier. In May 2005, Cleveland tight end Kellen Winslow Jr. nearly ended his football career when he was thrown from his motorcycle. As it turned out, he missed only the 2005 season before starting all 16 games in 2006.

THE SUPER STEELERS

Throughout the 1950s and '60s—heck, add the '30s and '40s to that too—it would've been absurd to think the Steelers could be playing for championships on a regular basis.

And after the team's 1–15 season in 1969, 5–9 in 1970, and 6–8 in '71, it was laughable to think the organization would soon be a perennial championship contender.

Funny how things worked out. By the time the Super Bowl years rolled around, starting with the 1974 season, losing at any time during the year was unacceptable. And the Super Bowl? Well, getting there not only was the focus, it also was the expectation.

"[The Super Bowl] was just another game, but to win that meant you were the best," said Dwight White, who played on the team's first four championship teams. "It's hard to explain, but if you start in September and play every down, by the time you go through the playoffs, and you finally get there, yeah, it's a big game. Then you just want to hurry up and get it over with. But it's a competitive thing. High strung is the phrase I like to use because I think that's really what we were—really wired guys in a positive type of way."

SUPER BOWL IX: WINNING ONE FOR THE CHIEF

There's something to be said about your first time. Regardless of what you're doing for that first time, it's memorable and something you don't want to miss. Riding a bike. Driving a car. Going on a date. Eating at Primanti Brothers. Having a child. In many cases, besides it being the first time, it might be the only time.

That's especially true in the world of sports, where you don't know if you'll ever get a second chance at a championship. Your first time very well could be your only time.

For the Steelers heading into Super Bowl IX, it meant reaching a championship game. *Finally*. They had appeared poised to get this far before. In 1972 there was the "Immaculate Reception" win over Oakland before losing in the AFC Championship Game to Miami. Then, in '73, a wild-card loss at Oakland. But they were improving.

Then, finally, after playoff wins over Buffalo and Oakland, Pittsburgh reached football's promised land.

Of course, the Minnesota Vikings were the exception to the "first-time" rule heading into Super Bowl IX. They had been there before. Twice, to be exact. Only they were still looking for their first win. After losses in those two games—to Kansas City in Super Bowl IV and Miami in Super Bowl VIII—the Vikings were thinking this time might be the charm.

Although the Steelers featured a potent offense behind the still-young Terry Bradshaw and the Vikings could put points on the board with Fran Tarkenton, each team's defense was something to behold. The Vikings and their Purple People Eaters. And, of course, the Steel Curtain.

In fact, on a cold afternoon in New Orleans (42 degrees with an announced 22-degree windchill), defense dominated the first half. The only points during the first two quarters came on a safety, thanks largely to Dwight "Mad Dog" White, who had missed nearly all of that week's preparation because he was in the hospital with pleurisy and viral pneumonia.

The record books all tell you that White sacked Tarkenton for Pittsburgh's first points in Super Bowl history. Just to be fair, though, it wasn't the type of head-jarring sack White usually got on opposing quarterbacks. He more or less just touched Tarkenton, who was down trying to recover a fumbled handoff.

"Despite what a lot of people think, I was the one who sacked [Tarkenton]," said White, laughing. "Most of the photos, however, show Jack Lambert standing over Tarkenton. But if you look at the record books, I'm credited with the safety. If you look at the pictures, it looks like Lambert sacked him because I'm not

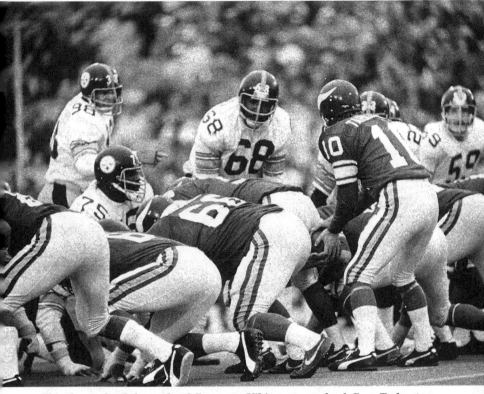

This shows the defense that Minnesota Vikings quarterback Fran Tarkenton had to face during Super Bowl IX on January 12, 1975, in New Orleans. The Pittsburgh Steelers in view are Ed Bradley (38), Joe Greene (75), L.C. Greenwood (68), and Jack Ham (59).

even in the picture. A miscarriage of justice."

Every member of the Steel Curtain was fantastic, pressuring Tarkenton the entire game and forcing turnovers.

Ultimately, turnovers played a big part in Super Bowl IX. In addition to the play that led to White's safety, with the Steelers leading 2–0 at halftime, Minnesota's Bill Brown fumbled the third-quarter opening kickoff and Marv Kellum recovered it for Pittsburgh. Four plays later, the Steelers reached the end zone on a nine-yard run by Franco Harris, who ended the game with 158 yards on 34 carries. Harris was selected as the game's Most Valuable Player.

The MVP award could've gone to the entire Pittsburgh

defense. The Steelers held the Viking offense to only 17 yards rushing (102 in the air) and no points offensively. Minnesota's only points came on Terry Brown's touchdown after Matt Blair blocked a Bobby Walden punt in the third quarter.

Of course, the award probably could have gone to "Mean" Joe Greene, who was relentless against Tarkenton and had one of the best games of his career. Earlier that season, Greene lined up differently to throw off opponents' blocking schemes, as if he were blocked effectively anyway. The Vikings didn't know how to stop him. They couldn't. In addition to the countless times Greene and his mates pressured the scrambling Tarkenton, Greene tipped and intercepted a Tarkenton pass as the Vikings were trying to drive in the third quarter.

Early in the fourth quarter, with the Vikings trying to score from the Pittsburgh 5-yard line, Greene recovered a fumble by Minnesota running back Chuck Foreman. That preserved Pittsburgh's 9–0 lead.

"That was the biggest defensive play of the day," said Chuck Noll. "They tried to run a counter play and Greene knocked the ball out of Foreman's hands. If they had scored then, they would have made it tough on us."

"They were just too good defensively," said Tarkenton. "You don't score many runs when [Sandy] Koufax is pitching."

Fittingly, after Bradshaw hit Larry Brown for a four-yard touchdown play late in the game, the Pittsburgh defense sealed the win for the Steelers when Mike Wagner picked off a Tarkenton pass. The Steelers held on for the 16–6 victory.

The title, the first of its kind for the Steelers, helped solidify the city of Pittsburgh's importance in the sports world at the time. After all, the Pirates had won baseball's World Series just a few years earlier in 1971, and the Pitt Panthers won the NCAA national football championship in 1976, the same year that Pitt's Tony Dorsett won the Heisman Trophy.

But no one from Pittsburgh could have been more proud than the Chief, Art Rooney, who, for 41 years, had watched the Steelers wallow in mediocrity. But he kept his same friendly, low-key demeanor the entire time.

In those days of postgame rituals inside the locker room, the team captains picked who would receive a game ball. Defensive captain Andy Russell stepped up to the platform to present the ball to "Mean" Joe Greene because, as Russell says, Greene was "devastating" against the Vikings. But then something happened.

"I saw the Chief standing in the background," Russell added. "He was just standing there, absorbing the atmosphere. I had a flashback to 1963 when we lost to the Giants and he went around and shook everybody's hands, thanking them for a great season. I immediately decided the ball had to go to the Chief."

And to think, this wasn't the only time the Chief would hold a Super Bowl trophy. There would be three more chances in the next five years. Who knew?

SUPER BOWL X: SWANN SOMEHOW FLIES

The similarities were night and day. Like jazz and country. Or Oscar and Felix. It was the blue-collar grit toughness of the Steelers against the flashy "America's Team" Cowboys. The Steelers not only didn't like hearing the Cowboys referred to in such a way; they loathed it.

"I think a lot of us—in fact I know I did, and I feel most of the Steelers did—took it personally," said cornerback Mel Blount. "Who granted them to be America's team?"

"When I think of Dallas, I think of El Dorados and Sevilles," said Dwight White. "We have El Dorados and Sevilles in Pittsburgh, too. But the salt on the roads has eaten big holes in them."

But then there was Chuck Noll versus Tom Landry. Terry Bradshaw versus Roger Staubach. The Steel Curtain versus the flex Doomsday. And, much like Super Bowl IX, each team's defense made the big plays.

To many, though, the most memorable performance in the game was the play of Steelers receiver Lynn Swann. And for good reason. Swann made some of the most acrobatic catches ever seen in a postseason game, before or since.

Funny, but Swann almost didn't play in the game. In the AFC Championship Game two weeks before the Super Bowl, Oakland's

George Atkinson belted Swann with a vicious hit in the back of the head with his fist. Even today the moment evokes several memories from the AFC Championship Game because as Swann lay on the field unconscious, teammate Joe Greene ran over and carefully carried him off the field. It looked oddly like a father carrying his sleeping son off to bed.

Swann, who suffered a concussion because of the incident, spent two days in the hospital after the game. He was doubtful for the Dallas game.

"In practices during the week before the Super Bowl, I was dropping passes left and right; my timing was off, and my concentration was awful," Swann said. "It didn't look as if the doctors were going to clear me to play, but shortly before the game I got the thumbs-up."

Good thing. Swann helped spark the Steeler offense.

Pittsburgh, down 7–0 after a Staubach to Drew Pearson touchdown play in the first quarter, put a drive together. During the next series, which ended with a seven-yard pass play from Bradshaw to Randy Grossman for a touchdown, Swann made a remarkable catch in front of the Pittsburgh bench. Bradshaw threw a pass near the sideline that looked like it was headed for the first row of seats. But Swann reached high over defender Mark Washington, caught the ball, and twisted his body perfectly so his feet landed inbounds for the 32-yard reception.

Swann has said that was the catch that shook the cobwebs from the concussion.

"Terry had called a play where I would go 10 or 15 yards and turn out, and when we lined up, the Cowboys covered me with Washington," Swann said. "I looked and saw the Cowboys were threatening to blitz.

"This wasn't the best play to run under those circumstances. I was almost expecting Terry to audible, but he stuck with the play."

The most famous play from Super Bowl X, the most famous catch in Swann's career, came in the second quarter.

Bradshaw, with one foot in his own end zone, lofted a pass to midfield. Swann dove away from Washington, tipped the ball, and then caught it with his fingertips as he was rolling onto his back. The play was good for 53 yards. The Steelers didn't score on the drive, but the play possibly set up Swann for a bigger play late in the game.

"I still don't know how I caught it," Swann said of the 53-yard grab. "I don't know how I kept my concentration on the ball while I was going down. After that, I started feeling my confidence return, and I was ready to have a big game."

Swann indeed had a big game. Sort of. Swann, who was picked as the game's Most Valuable Player, finished with 161 receiving yards and one touchdown. But he caught only four passes.

Besides being able to have one of his most spectacular displays during the biggest game of the year, Swann was able to face a challenge head-on too. Dallas free safety Cliff Harris, a fearless hitter, had issued a warning for Swann through the media during the week.

"The hungry reporters asked me if I was going to take it easy on [Swann]," Harris said. "I told them only logically, 'Fellows, we choose this profession of football and we realize…it is a rough sport. Swann's health is not up to me. It is up to Lynn. If he comes into my area, it is his choice and I will not be thinking about his last week's concussion. If Lynn doesn't want to endanger his health, then he shouldn't play or at least he should not come into my area.' It was a statement of fact, not a threat."

Harris, even though he had his chances, never got the cheap shot on Swann that he wanted. But he wasn't free from controversy.

In the third quarter, the Steelers found themselves in field-goal range, trailing 10–7, after picking off a Roger Staubach pass. Kicker Roy Gerela, who had missed a field-goal try near the end of the first half, was called on for a 33-yard attempt. He missed it left.

When the ball sailed to the left, Harris gave Gerela a little hug and a tap on the helmet. Pittsburgh linebacker Jack Lambert, standing a few feet away, took offense to it. Lambert grabbed Harris by the shoulder pads and tossed him to the ground.

"The referee or the umpire said to me, 'You're out; you're out of here,'" said Lambert. "I said 'Wait a minute, this is the Super Bowl; you can't throw me out of this game.' He said, 'Then you get back in that huddle and you shut up.' I said, 'Yes sir.'"

Lambert ended up having a huge game for the Steelers, recording 14 tackles. After feeling the Steelers were being intimidated by

Dallas in the first half, Lambert became the enforcer. In addition to the Harris incident, Lambert also got into a tussle with former Steelers teammate Preston Pearson.

"[The Steelers] started controlling our offense in the second half behind the play of [Lambert]," Staubach said in 2000. "He wasn't really somebody that I liked, but I respected him. I still get mad at our players for not reacting when Lambert kicked Preston Pearson on the ground, but he fired up the Steelers. He made it happen. He was the glue in that defense."

Although many point to Lambert as the spark the Steelers needed, that's not completely the case. The momentum-changer came a few minutes into the fourth quarter.

The Cowboys, leading 10–7, were forced to punt from their own 16 with 11:28 remaining in the game. Reggie Harrison, Pittsburgh's backup fullback, busted through the Dallas line and blocked Mitch Hoopes's punt.

"I never blocked a punt before in my life," said Harrison. "I charged in and hit the upback with my arm. Then there was nobody in front of me, and Hoopes had just taken his first step. There was no way they could stop me. I tried to hit it down, so I could fall on it for six points. All I was thinking about was six points."

Instead, the ball went out of the end zone for a safety. But the Steelers had new life.

Over the next five minutes, the Steelers got two field goals from Gerela, from 36 and 18 yards, respectively, and took a 15–10 lead. The 36-yarder gave Pittsburgh its first lead of the game. The Steelers didn't trail again.

The Steelers practically put the finishing touches on the Cowboys with three minutes left when Bradshaw launched another pass down the middle of the field to Swann for a 64-yard touchdown. Bradshaw got hammered on the play and didn't return.

Dallas, not willing to concede the game, went 80 yards in a little more than a minute, and cut the score to 21–17 when Percy Howard caught a Staubach pass for a 34-yard touchdown. That would be the only pass Howard, who played basketball rather than football in college, caught during his NFL career.

With Terry Hanratty in at quarterback for Pittsburgh, the

Steelers stalled near midfield and went for it on fourth down. The gamble didn't pay off. Staubach and the Cowboys got the ball on their own 39 with a little more than a minute left. Plenty of time and weapons for Staubach in most circumstances. Of course, most defenses weren't Pittsburgh's.

Staubach got Dallas to the Pittsburgh 38 with less than 10 seconds remaining. On the game's final play, Staubach threw up a "Hail Mary." Mike Wagner batted the ball into the hands of Pittsburgh teammate Glen Edwards. The Steelers had their second consecutive NFL championship.

"I felt that we could have won if we had used our time more wisely," said Staubach. "It's funny; we spent more time working on the two-minute drill during the rest of my career, largely because we didn't use the clock effectively in that Super Bowl.

"Take nothing away from Pittsburgh, though. The famed Steel Curtain defense of the Steelers was fantastic. They totally shut down our running attack in that game, and for the most part, shut down our wide receivers. We had to scramble to make plays."

The Steelers had become the third team to repeat as Super Bowl champs, joining Green Bay and Miami.

Said linebackers coach Woody Widenhofer, a Butler, Pennsylvania, native who would become the defensive coordinator for the team's next two Super Bowls, "I don't think we actually realized we were with one of the best teams ever until after [Super Bowl X] was over.... As years go on you really thank God you had a chance to be part of history."

SUPER BOWL XIII: BRADSHAW SPELLS "MVP"

Terry Bradshaw wasn't ever accused of being the sharpest tool in the shed throughout his career, even at Super Bowl XIII, at the end of Bradshaw's eighth year in the league.

By anyone not pulling for the Steelers, Bradshaw was seen as a hick from Louisiana. Some in Pittsburgh even questioned his intelligence, especially during his first few years with the Steelers.

The NFL's top draft pick out of Louisiana Tech in 1970, Bradshaw has admitted that he had trouble reading NFL

Terry Bradshaw smiles after leading his team to a 35–31 victory over the Dallas Cowboys in Super Bowl XIII in Miami on January 21, 1979. Bradshaw fired four touchdown passes, broke two Super Bowl passing records, and was named the game's MVP.

TRIVIA

During the Steelers' first four Super Bowl titles in the 1970s, how many playoff games did they have to play on the road (excluding Super Bowls)?

Find the answers on pages 165–166.

defenses early in his career. That's partly the reason, he says, that he threw 24 interceptions in 1970 and then 22 the next year. He simply made some rookie mistakes. It didn't help matters that head coach Chuck Noll showed little confidence in his young quarterback and, on at least one occasion, called Bradshaw "dummy."

In 1970, Bradshaw's first year, the Steelers started out 0–3, including losses at Denver and at Cleveland. Noll decided he needed to give Bradshaw and Terry Hanratty an equal shot at the starting job. Therefore, he tried a rotation with one quarterback playing one half and the other playing the second half.

"Any fool knows you can't do that with quarterbacks," Bradshaw said. "All rookie quarterbacks experience trauma. And even in those losses, I was gaining confidence. Had my coach been wise enough to understand that, he would have stayed with me."

Even though Bradshaw effectively beat out Hanratty and threw for a boatload of yards (3,669 in his first two seasons, to be exact), Noll kept challenging him. In 1972, the Steelers drafted quarterback Joe Gilliam in the 11th round. After the team's record improved to 11–3 and 10–4 over the next two seasons, Noll gave the job to Gilliam in 1974.

Finally, in 1975, whether in spite of or because of Noll's badgering, Bradshaw took over as the team's top quarterback.

"Being called dumb is the most deprecating term for a human to endure—not just a football player, but any human being," said Bradshaw. "Can you imagine the embarrassment that it caused my friends and family? Multiply it times a hundred and that's how it felt to me."

When the stage was the biggest in football, the Super Bowl, everything was magnified even more, including Bradshaw's intelligence or perceived lack of. Before Super Bowl IX, the organization's first shot at the title, Bradshaw was bombarded with questions about his IQ.

Then, in the days leading up to Super Bowl XIII against Dallas in Miami, Thomas "Hollywood" Henderson, an outspoken—if not downright cocky—linebacker for the Cowboys was asked about Bradshaw. Henderson replied: "Terry Bradshaw couldn't spell 'cat' if you spotted him the 'c' and the 'a.'"

Although the line gave Henderson additional recognition—after all, 30 years later it's still being mentioned—it didn't amuse Bradshaw. He did a wonderful job of playing along, though.

"I can too: C...A...T."

Of course, by the end of the game, Bradshaw proved that he could spell "touchdown" and "win" and "champions" and "MVP" too.

The game itself had all the markings of a classic matchup. The 14–2 Steelers and the 12–4 Cowboys. A rematch of Super Bowl X. Two-time Super Bowl champs facing the defending champs. The hype was there. Unlike many overly hyped games, however, this one lived up to its billing.

After John Banaszak recovered a Drew Pearson fumble on a double reverse during Dallas's opening drive, the Steelers struck quickly. Bradshaw found John Stallworth in the corner of the end zone for a 28-yard scoring strike barely five minutes into the game.

At the end of the quarter the Cowboys finally reached the end zone following a Bradshaw fumble. Staubach and Tony Hill hooked up for a 39-yard touchdown play as time ran out.

On the ensuing possession, the Steelers reached midfield before Mike Hegman stripped the ball from Bradshaw and returned it 37 yards for the Dallas lead.

Just like any classic heavyweight battle, though, the Steelers answered quickly. On their third play from scrimmage, Bradshaw threw a 10-yard pass to Stallworth on the sideline. Stallworth cut toward the middle of the field and then legged out the 75-yard scoring play.

As halftime approached, the Steelers moved the ball down the field again. Pittsburgh was facing a third-and-short at the Dallas 7-yard line. Bradshaw, who called all of his own plays during the game, wanted to run a quick play-action pass to Rocky Bleier.

"I was headed outside linebacker D.D. Lewis, who came across the line of scrimmage to take away my path," Bleier said. "All of a sudden with the broken play we had to become a little flexible, so I cut in and around Lewis, while Bradshaw spun to the outside and looked for other options. I drifted backward. He continued to his right with very little running room and it quickly became one of those moments where, *bam*, we spotted one another. I always tell people that it was a 'time stood still as our eyes met across the field' kind of moment.

"Terry threw the ball but it was so high I couldn't tell if it was supposed to be a pass or if he was throwing it away. I think, in all honesty, he was throwing it away because it was sailing over my head. In my thought process of going up, I thought I might be able to tip it. As I went up, though, I felt a *thud* of it sticking to my hands. I had it. I fell down in the end zone for the score."

Bleier's fantastic catch, which ended up giving the Steelers the lead for good, was captured for posterity as the *Sports Illustrated* cover shot that week, January 29.

In a game so well played by so many great players, teams look for every break they can catch. The Steelers got a potentially game-changing one in the third quarter.

With Pittsburgh still up 21–14, the Cowboys moved the ball down to the Steelers' 10. On third down, Staubach found a wide open Jackie Smith in the end zone. But Staubach hit the backup tight end Smith in a bad place—his hands—as Smith was tripping to the ground. Actually, the ball went through Smith's hands, bounced off his chest, and fell onto the painted end zone grass. Dallas had to settle for three points.

Midway through the fourth quarter, facing third-and-9 at the Dallas 22, Franco Harris plowed through the left side of the line and went in for the touchdown. After the Cowboys fumbled the ensuing kick, which Dennis Winston recovered, Bradshaw threw a perfect pass to Lynn Swann at the back of the end zone for an 18-yard touchdown.

Just like that, in 19 seconds, the Steelers led 35–17 with less than seven minutes to play.

But the Cowboys wouldn't go away. Staubach marched Dallas

A PICTURE ISN'T WORTH QUITE A THOUSAND WORDS

Dwight White was a key member of the Steel Curtain defense during the four Super Bowls of the 1970s. By the time the Steelers played in Super Bowl IX, White had been around for four years. He wasn't some rookie trying to be remembered or an aging veteran on his way out. No, White was entering the prime of his career.

So he was a little disappointed when he missed the team Super Bowl photo because he was stuck in the hospital with pleurisy and viral pneumonia. But that was just the half of it.

"What's worse is that they didn't even think enough to put my name on the damn photo saying I was there," said White with a tone that was a combination of tongue-in-cheek and being genuinely irked. "This was the first Pittsburgh team ever to go to the Super Bowl, I had been in the hospital all week and scored the first two points of the game. I was an inspiration and they didn't even think enough to put my name as missing.... But I got that championship ring."

down the field in eight plays and four minutes, 24 seconds before a seven-yard touchdown pass to Billy Joe DuPree.

Trailing 35–24 with 2:27 left to play, the Cowboys needed to try an onside kick. Noll put in his "hands" guys—receivers, running backs, defensive backs—to grab it for the Steelers. Rafael Septien's line-drive kick bounced off Tony Dungy and the Cowboys recovered.

Staubach worked quickly and eventually hit Butch Johnson for a four-yard scoring play with 22 seconds remaining. Time for another onside kick.

"Here's human nature for you," Bleier said. "Chuck puts in all of the hands people again. I started thinking to myself, 'Here we go, what's he going to do?' And then I suddenly started thinking, 'Don't kick it to me; don't kick it to me.' I was afraid of them drilling the ball instead of dribbling toward me and then me not getting a handle on it, much like what happened to Dungy the play before. Of course, Septien dribbled it. All I had to know was to not let it go 10 yards. So I moved up and fell on top of it. Guys started jumping on the pile above and around me. Knees were going into my back. Frankly, it was the hardest hit I had all day.

"But it was worth it. We had won."

The Steelers had become the first team to win three Super Bowls.

The "dummy" tag unfortunately stuck with Terry Bradshaw throughout his career. In the late 1990s, Bradshaw was diagnosed with clinical depression. Even with his personal demons, Bradshaw has had a football "afterlife" that many people, including those who questioned his intelligence, wouldn't mind having.

Bradshaw, who has written five books and recorded five singing albums, has appeared in several feature films and television series, including *Hooper, Cannonball Run, Failure to Launch,* and *Everybody Loves Raymond.* Bradshaw also owns Terry Bradshaw Quarter Horses and Circle 12 Ranch, plus he's co-owner of NASCAR's Fitz-Bradshaw Racing.

Bradshaw remains one of the most recognizable NFL television analysts, first with CBS Sports and currently with Fox Sports.

Oh, one footnote to Thomas "Hollywood" Henderson's infamous "cat" quote before Super Bowl XIII. Bradshaw played it up once again on another pretty big stage. In 1989, while making his induction speech for the Pro Football Hall of Fame, in a class that included Mel Blount, Bradshaw said, "Y'all called me 'Ozark Ike' 'cause I was big and white and dumb actin'. Said I was L'il Abner. Said I couldn't spell 'cat.' Well, y'all didn't, but some fool down in Dallas did."

In an interesting twist, in early 2001 Bradshaw sat down with the "fool" Henderson for a one-on-one interview for Fox's *NFL Sunday*.

"As I sat opposite him during that interview," Bradshaw said, "I certainly felt no animosity toward him."

By that time, Henderson's life had taken an ugly turn because of drug and alcohol abuse. Henderson, who's admitted he used cocaine during Super Bowl XIII, was out of football a few years after that game, and found himself in prison. By the time Bradshaw sat down with him, Henderson had turned his life around. He started the East Side Youth Services and Street

Outreach in Texas, and he began speaking to groups about the dangers of drugs. In March 2000, Henderson won $28 million in the Texas Lottery.

"I apologized to him and he said that's okay," Henderson told the *Fort Worth Star-Telegram* in 2007. "I knew that it hurt him, and it pained him to be labeled dumb. But I know he has made millions on that."

For his fantastic play in Super Bowl XIII, including 318 passing yards and a record four touchdowns while calling all of his own plays, Bradshaw received the game's Most Valuable Player award.

"Super Bowl XIII was the most pressure-packed game I ever played in," Bradshaw wrote in his 1989 book, *Going Deep*. He later added, "I honestly felt I had finally joined the elite among NFL quarterbacks after winning my third Super Bowl."

If Super Bowl XIII didn't put him in a select crowd, Super Bowl XIV certainly did.

By the time Bradshaw retired after the 1983 season, he had amassed 27,989 yards passing and 212 touchdowns. Also, he had led the Steelers to eight AFC Central Division championships and four Super Bowl titles, and he was selected as the Super Bowl MVP two times. Not bad for someone who couldn't spell "cat."

SUPER BOWL XIV: CHAMPS ESCAPE WITH FOURTH TITLE

By the end of the 1979 season, the Steelers were showing their age. The Steel Curtain was no longer impenetrable.

During the 12–4 season, the Steelers still dominated teams, but they did it more with offense. In fact, behind Bradshaw's 3,724 yards passing and Franco Harris's 1,186 yards rushing, the Steelers led the NFL in scoring with 416 points. The defense, which had ranked first in two of the previous three seasons, was now ranked fifth in the league.

The offense was so potent that it scored 51 points in an October game at Cleveland. They hadn't hung 50 points on a team since scoring 55 against...well, Cleveland (in 1954).

So, losing a defensive step or not, after beating rival Houston in the AFC Championship Game, 27–13, the NFC representative to the Super Bowl, a surprise Los Angeles team, looked like a pushover.

Sure, the Los Angeles Rams were on a bit of a hot streak, reaching the Super Bowl by upsetting defending NFC champs Dallas and then Tampa Bay. Plus they had three former Steelers' coaches on their staff: Lionel Taylor, Dan Radakovich, and the man behind the Steel Curtain, Bud Carson. Not to mention the Super Bowl would be played in Pasadena, not far (a long Matt Bahr field goal, maybe) from the Rams' home.

Frankly, the Rams weren't supposed to get this far. They were 9–7, for crying out loud. The Steelers were supposed to reach the title game. Even though there were some chinks in their armor, they remained the veteran-full, three-time Super Bowl champion Steelers. The oddsmakers in Vegas had Pittsburgh as a double-digit favorite, anywhere from 10–14 points.

Something odd happened, though. The Rams weren't intimidated. Just the opposite. They seemed to think they could beat the Steelers.

"Bud [Carson] had us playing in a team format," said Rams veteran defensive end Jack Youngblood, who showed his team's resolve by playing with a broken leg. "And we knew that we could match up helmet-to-helmet with their guys—their first line against our first line—and it wasn't any big deal.

"The thing that I remember was that we were the big underdogs. As a football team we didn't believe that. The core of us didn't and we knew we could go in there and play with them. We just didn't have the quarterback who could take that game and take charge of that game like Terry [Bradshaw]."

But L.A. quarterback Vince Ferragamo—a backup who played during the year because starter Pat Haden was injured—wasn't exactly a slouch, at least not against the Steelers.

Ferragamo, who threw for 212 yards in the contest, and a stingy Ram defense stunned the Steeler-partisan crowd of 103,985 by taking a 13–10 lead at halftime.

"As strange as this may sound, I believe that game was won at halftime," said Bahr, a rookie kicker that year who put the Steelers

Lynn Swann, John Stallworth, and Franco Harris watch the action while the Steelers defense is on the field against the Los Angeles Rams in Super Bowl XIV in Pasadena on January 21, 1980. All three scored touchdowns in the Steelers' 31–19 win.

on the board first in the opening quarter with a 41-yard field goal. "There were many great plays and players in the game, but Jack Lambert (a man of few words) and Joe Greene (a man of many words) gave a halftime tongue-lashing to all that were present. It was a wakeup call that we all needed."

Early in the third quarter, the Steelers took the lead on a 47-yard pass play from Bradshaw to Lynn Swann. The lead was short lived. The Rams scored on their next possession thanks to a 24-yard halfback touchdown pass from Lawrence McCutcheon to Ron Smith.

As they had done after the second quarter, the Rams shocked nearly everyone by taking a 19–17 lead into the final period. Finally, early in the fourth quarter, the Steelers took the lead for good on the game's most memorable play. On third-and-eight from their own 27, Bradshaw threw a perfect pass to the Rams 32-yard line and the outstretched arms of John Stallworth, who beat Rod Perry and glided the rest of the way for a touchdown.

"I didn't like the call," Bradshaw said after the game, "but you know, the coach sent it in. I hadn't been hitting that pass all week. It's a matter of building confidence. You don't build confidence in things that don't work. Maybe it was our ace in the hole. I don't know."

Stallworth finished the game with 121 yards receiving on three catches.

Evidently that touchdown, with a little more than 12 minutes left, was the ace in the hole. In a game that included six lead changes, the Steelers didn't look back after going up 24–19.

Fittingly, a defensive play locked up the game for the Steelers late in the fourth quarter with Pittsburgh still leading 24–19. Los Angeles was driving in Pittsburgh territory when for some reason Lambert dropped back in coverage and intercepted a Ferragamo pass at the Steelers' 14.

That was Ferragamo's only interception of the day, compared to Bradshaw's three. But Bradshaw threw for 309 yards and two touchdowns en route to his second-straight Super Bowl MVP.

The Steelers added a final touchdown—a one-yard run by Franco Harris with one minute, 49 seconds remaining—and escaped their fourth and final Super Bowl of the dynasty with a 31–19 win. Along the way, Pittsburgh became the first team to win four Super Bowls.

As Bahr wrote in the book *Super Bowl Sunday*, "Even champions sometimes get lucky."

The team's mantra in 1980 was to "win one for the thumb." The organization would have to wait more than 25 years for that fifth ring. But there's no denying their dominance for a decade.

"The Pittsburgh team from the seventies is probably the best of all time," said Ferragamo. "Cumulatively, between offense and defense and special teams and coaches and owners, I put them up against any team."

SUPER BOWL XL: THE BUS STOPS HERE

It's not often that a player gets an opportunity to end his career perfectly. Baseball Hall of Famer Ted Williams homered in his last at-bat. UCLA basketball coach John Wooden ended his coaching career with his Bruins winning the national championship.

And on February 5, 2006, Jerome Bettis ended his 13-year NFL career in grand fashion: a Super Bowl championship in his hometown of Detroit as the Steelers handled the Seattle Seahawks, 21–10.

For the two weeks between Pittsburgh's unlikely 34–17 dismantling of the Denver Broncos in the Mile-High City and Super Bowl XL, much of the pregame fodder centered around Bettis.

He was the perfect sidebar. In many ways, that was perfect. Bettis made a great sidebar to the game—the biggest of his career—and it was being played less than 10 miles from where he starred at David Mackenzie High School.

Even the team knew what was happening. Quarterback Ben Roethlisberger boldly promised to Bettis after the 2004 season that if Bettis would hold off retirement for one more year, Big Ben would do everything in his power to help the Steelers reach the Super Bowl.

When the team boarded the plane for Detroit, Bettis noticed teammate Joey Porter handing out green No. 6 Notre Dame

---

DID YOU KNOW...

Steelers' punter Craig Colquitt (1978–81 and 1983–84) is part of a family tree of punters? His brother, Jimmy, punted for Seattle in 1985. One of his sons, Dustin, was a third-round pick by Kansas City in 2005. His other son, Britton, was a 2007 All-SEC selection at punter as a junior at Tennessee.

---

jerseys—replicas of Bettis's from college.

"I didn't get the true extent of it until I got on the plane and I saw how many jerseys there actually were," Bettis said. "When I got on the plane there were dozens. I was taken aback by how much they thought of me to give me that kind of tribute. That was a special feeling, knowing that they wanted to do that for me."

The entire city of Pittsburgh would've done it, if possible. After all, Bettis, one of the Steelers' all-time best trade acquisitions, had become the face of the franchise. There had been great players—Rod Woodson, Carnell Lake, Greg Lloyd, Louis Lipps, and Barry Foster, to name a few—before and after the Steelers got Bettis from the St. Louis Rams on draft day in 1996 in exchange for draft choices. But Bettis was the Steelers' "Mr. Everything."

He ran for 10,571 yards in 10 seasons with the Steelers, good for second on the team's all-time list. He has more 100-yard rushing games (50) than any other Steeler. Off the field, he hosted a popular television show in Pittsburgh and started the Bus Stops Here Foundation for underprivileged children. And he did nearly everything with that wide grin on his face.

Indeed, the city, the organization, and his teammates did whatever possible to help "the Bus" finish his career well at Detroit's Super Bowl.

The instance on the airplane was one of two times before the game itself that Porter would let Bettis soak in the moment. The other happened as the team was getting set to run onto Ford Field for the game introductions. Porter held his teammates back at the end of the tunnel and asked Bettis to lead the team out.

SUPER BOWL IX

Tulane Stadium
New Orleans, Louisiana
January 12, 1975
Minnesota   0 0 0 6— 6
Pittsburgh   0 2 7 7—16
Attendance: 80,997
MVP: Franco Harris

SUPER BOWL X

Orange Bowl
Miami, Florida
January 18, 1976
Dallas 7 3 0 7—17
Pittsburgh 7 0 0 14—21
Attendance: 80,187
MVP: Lynn Swann

SUPER BOWL XIII

Orange Bowl
Miami, Florida
January 21, 1979
Dallas   7 7 3 14—31
Pittsburgh   7 14 0 14—35
Attendance: 79,484
MVP: Terry Bradshaw

SUPER BOWL XIV

Rose Bowl
Pasadena, California
January 20, 1980
Los Angeles 7 6 6 0—19
Pittsburgh 3 7 7 14—31
Attendance: 103,985
MVP: Terry Bradshaw

SUPER BOWL XL

Ford Field
Detroit, Michigan
February 5, 2006
Seattle 3 0 7 0—10
Pittsburgh 0 7 7 7—21
Attendance: 68,206
MVP: Hines Ward

All sorts of emotions were going through Bettis's head as he began his run-dance past the banners of the previous Super Bowls' Most Valuable Players. This was it. The final time he'd run onto the field before a game. And he was doing it in Detroit. For the Super Bowl.

"I was screaming and going crazy and have never been so jacked up in my life," he said. "I tried to take in as much as I could, but when I came out I was so emotional I didn't see everything. But I did see that crowd, and I saw how electric they were. The Terrible Towels were everywhere. I was so surprised how many fans we had there. I could have never envisioned that moment. I didn't know if we'd ever get to the Super Bowl, much less a Super Bowl in my own hometown."

BRADSHAW, STAUBACH, IT'S EASY TO CONFUSE THE TWO

It's relatively easy to look at Terry Bradshaw and Roger Staubach and tell the two apart. It always has been. Well, for most everyone.

See, following Pittsburgh's win over Dallas in Super Bowl X, Terry Bradshaw was invited to the White House to meet President Gerald Ford and Vice President Nelson Rockefeller. Bradshaw wanted to impress the woman he was dating, so he asked (as he puts it) his "future second ex-wife to be," Olympic skater Jo Jo Starbuck, to come along.

According to Bradshaw in his book *It's Only a Game*, Vice President Rockefeller must've had a momentary brain lapse.

The vice president was very kind to me. "You know, fella," he said, "you're the best quarterback I've ever seen..."

Wow!

"...I've always enjoyed watching how cool you are under pressure..."

Aw, shucks.

"...and you're definitely a role model to the young people of this country..."

Hope you're listening to this, Jo Jo.

"Why, from that first game I saw you play at the Naval Academy..."

Uh-oh.

"...and when the Cowboys drafted you I thought..."

Obviously the vice president had heard the name Starbuck and decided I was Roger Staubach, the Dallas Cowboys quarterback, who had not won Super Bowl X.

I didn't know what to do. It was terribly embarrassing, particularly in front of the woman I desperately wanted to impress. I finally realized I had no choice. After a few agonizing moments I stood up tall and straight, put my arm protectively around Jo Jo's shoulders, and said proudly, "Did you see that game we played against Army my senior year?"

If the vice president of the United States of America wanted me to be Roger Staubach, I was going to be the best possible Roger Staubach for the rest of the evening.

The game itself, though, turned out to be much more than Bettis. Much more. In fact, Bettis and his 43 yards were less than spectacular. If it weren't for the fact that he was Mr. Steeler playing his final game at a Super Bowl in his hometown, Bettis would've been just another player in the box score.

The same could be said for second-year quarterback Ben Roethlisberger, who looked more like Ben Stiller trying to play at times. Roethlisberger finished with a 22.6 passer rating, the lowest ever for a Super Bowl-winning quarterback, after completing 9-of-21 passes for 123 yards, throwing two critical interceptions, and throwing no passing touchdowns.

"We got the win, and that's all that matters," Roethlisberger said afterward. "It was absolutely awesome to come up here and win one for Jerome."

With Big Ben and the Bus relatively ineffective, Super Bowl XL proved to be a great place for Hines Ward to shine and show that he was not only one of the Steelers' difference-makers, but he also was one of the top players in the NFL.

After the entire Pittsburgh offense looked lethargic during its first four possessions, the Steelers finally got things going late in the second quarter. Trailing 3–0 after a 47-yard field goal by Seattle's Josh Brown at the end of the opening period, Ward started it with a 12-yard scamper on a shovel pass from Roethlisberger.

Later in the drive, facing a third-and-28 from the Seattle 40, Roethlisberger made possibly his best play of the night. Seattle forced Roethlisberger out of the pocket. He looked like he was going to take off running—which he did seven times during the game for 25 yards—but instead he stopped just shy of the line of scrimmage, ran sideways, and then found Ward for a 37-yard pickup.

Three plays later, Big Ben ran it in from the 1, giving the Steelers their first lead of the game, with 1:55 left in the half. On the touchdown, it appeared to some that Roethlisberger didn't reach the end zone before going down, which would've put the Steelers at fourth down. After a review, referee Bill Leavy upheld the ruling on the field. The Steelers didn't trail again.

The Steelers took what appeared to be a commanding lead early in the second half. On the second play from scrimmage, the

Jerome Bettis (right) and Super Bowl XL MVP Hines Ward celebrate after the trophy ceremony after the Steelers' 21–10 win over the Seattle Seahawks in Super Bowl XL on February 5, 2006, in Detroit.

Pittsburgh offensive line—Alan Faneca, Max Starks, and Kendall Simmons—opened a huge hole for halfback Willie Parker, who surged for a 75-yard touchdown run. It was the longest run in Super Bowl history. More important, it helped put the Steelers up 14–3.

On their next possession, it looked like the Steelers were about to break the game open. Pittsburgh had moved the ball down the field to the Seattle 7, facing a third down. The Steelers would get at least three points out of the deal, right?

Not exactly. Roethlisberger threw one of his ill-timed interceptions when his lame-duck pass dropped into the arms of Seattle cornerback Kelly Herndon, who went 76 yards to the Pittsburgh 20. The Seahawks scored quickly and cut the Pittsburgh lead to 14–10.

Seattle had a chance to take the lead early in the fourth quarter. The Seahawks were inside the Pittsburgh "red zone." Quarterback Matt Hasselbeck and tight end Jerramy Stevens hooked up for an 18-yard play that put Seattle on the 1. Or so it seemed. A holding call against right tackle Sean Locklear pushed the ball back. Two plays later, Ike Taylor picked off a Hasselbeck pass for Pittsburgh.

Adding to Seattle's frustration, the Steelers ran a trick play during the ensuing possession. Wide receiver Antwaan Randle El, who had been a quarterback at Indiana University, threw a perfect strike to Ward, who finished off the 43-yard touchdown play that gave the Steelers a 21–10 lead with eight minutes, 56 seconds left in the game.

"I was so open," Ward said, "that I just kept thinking, 'Please, ball get here, huh!' It just seemed like it happened in such slow motion, you know? But it was a great play call, at just the right time, something that we had run before and had some success with, and it worked again.

"It was kind of typical of the night. We sputtered some, and gave the ball away a few times, but we made big plays. And big plays in big games is what it's all about."

Ward was selected as the game's MVP with 123 yards receiving and one touchdown on five catches.

It's easy to point to Super Bowl XL as the elusive "one for the thumb," Pittsburgh's fifth NFL championship, joining San Francisco and Dallas.

But these Steelers did it unlike any of the other four title teams. They never were expected to dominate. They had a solid defense, but it wasn't the Steel Curtain. They had playmakers on offense, but they weren't viewed in the same light as Bradshaw, Harris, Bleier, Swann, and Stallworth.

The 2005 Steelers weren't the same as their counterparts from a quarter-century earlier. But they showed that they were one of football's best. A team that could find itself on football's biggest stage again in upcoming years.

Of course they'd be doing it without Bettis, who stood on the makeshift stage at Ford Field, kissed and hoisted the Lombardi Trophy for everyone to see, and announced his retirement.

"It's been an incredible ride," Bettis told the enthusiastic crowd, which included his parents, Johnnie and Gladys, who missed only two of Jerome's professional games in person. "I played this game to win a championship. I'm a champion, and I think the Bus's last stop is here in Detroit.

"Detroit, you were incredible. Pittsburgh, here we come."

LEADING THE WAY

The Steelers have had their fair share of coaches throughout their history. Some could've been good if given a chance. But with others, a season was long enough. Excluding longtime coach Bill Cowher, who's been the subject of a few books, the two coaches who turned the "Same Old Steelers" into a dynasty were Chuck Noll and Bud Carson.

CHUCK NOLL: CHANGING A CULTURE

Rocky Bleier remembers the moment in 1974 when he realized the "genius" of Chuck Noll. The Steelers had just beaten the Kansas City Chiefs in Kansas City, 34–24. With the win, Pittsburgh improved to 3–1–1 on the season.

Because of injuries to Franco Harris and Frenchy Fuqua, Bleier got his first start of the season that game. It gave him a chance to go up against a Chiefs defense that included aging veterans and future Hall of Famers such as Bobby Bell and Buck Buchanan. The Steelers defense, coming into its own as the Steel Curtain, sacked quarterback Len Dawson three times.

During the film session on the Tuesday after the game, Bleier determined what type of coach the Steelers had in Noll.

Noll pointed out that the reason the Steelers were able to get to Dawson three times was because of Kansas City's left guard, Ed Budde.

"He was an All-Pro going up against Hall of Famer Buck

Chuck Noll poses with Terry Bradshaw, the top draft choice of the Pittsburgh Steelers, at a Pittsburgh news conference in February 1970. The Louisiana Tech quarterback was in town to discuss salary terms with the club.

DID YOU KNOW...

Each player on the Super Bowl XIII and XIV Pittsburgh teams was a true Steeler? Much like coach Chuck Noll's idea when he started as head coach, the players on those Steelers teams had played professionally for only Pittsburgh.

Buchanan every day in practice," Bleier remembers of Noll's assessment. "Rather than staying in front of my man, it's easier to let him go through. Chuck pointed out that was the reason we beat the Kansas City Chiefs.

"As I'm hearing this, I couldn't believe it. He broke it down to this one tiny detail. I figured if he could do that, I was buying into it. Chuck and his coaching staff never took a shortcut."

By that time in 1974, Noll had already proven that he knew what it would take to turn this organization around. Shoot, he pretty much announced it when he took over the job in 1969 from Bill Austin.

At the end of the 1960s, the "Same Old Steelers" had placed an emphasis on "Old." They were pitiful and full of tired, cynical veterans with an attitude. As the story goes, in the first meeting with his team Noll said that after watching game film, he could tell why the Steelers kept losing.

"You could've heard a pin drop," said veteran linebacker Andy Russell, "because we had tried figuring it out and obviously couldn't. He said, basically, 'It has nothing to do with your attitude. The problem is that you're not any good.'"

Those were bold words for a young first-time head coach. Especially one without a lot of expectations, which is obvious in the January 18, 1969, *Pittsburgh Post-Gazette*:

"Chuck Noll is no miracle man, but the husky 37-year-old six-footer gives the impression of being eager to try to pump some winning fluid into the Steelers.

"The former Baltimore Colts' assistant coach made a fine first appearance here yesterday at the Roosevelt Hotel, only a few

TRIVIA

Who did the Steelers beat
for Bill Cowher's 100th
coaching win?

Find the answers on pages 165–166.

hours after he was named to succeed Bill Austin.

"Noll had no immediate plans to win any titles for the Steelers, who never have won a championship, but he has three years to build a winner.

"He's a good speaker, gives you the idea he's a solid man, and appears to be confident without being boastful. He owns a good football mind and a memory to match."

Originally, Noll was seen as too young at 37 for the Pittsburgh job. So Dan Rooney had offered it to Penn State coach Joe Paterno, who turned it down. As Rooney looked around the league for an assistant who might be ready, Chuck Noll's name kept popping up.

Of that first meeting with the Steelers, Russell added that Noll continued to tell the team that, in essence, he was going to be getting rid of the dead weight. Players who didn't fit his system would be sent packing, and players who understood what he wanted to accomplish would play. In other words, the old, cynical guys were going to be giving way to rookies who could be molded. And that's exactly what happened.

Beginning with that year's draft, Noll put his permanent mark on the organization when he drafted "Mean" Joe Greene out of North Texas State. That was about the only positive to come out of the '69 season, as the Steelers won their first game and then proceeded to lose the remaining 13.

Noll wasn't used to losing, but he knew it would take time to save the Steelers. Noll started his playing career in the NFL as a guard with Cleveland, 1953–59, before moving to linebacker. While with the Browns, Noll played in four NFL championship games, winning two of them.

"Without being trite, he was a coach who could coach all positions or have a working knowledge of all of them," said Bleier. "He was the defensive coordinator of the Colts but he was an offensive guard as a player. He commanded respect. And he always had a well-thought, basic answer.

DID YOU KNOW...

The Steelers beat the New England Patriots in both Chuck Noll's 100th and 200th wins as a head coach? The 100th came in the 1979 season opener, a 16–13 overtime win. The 200th came on December 9, 1990, when the Steelers beat the Patriots 24–3 at home.

"He set the expectations high when he first came in, but it elevated the expectations of the players."

Sure enough, with an unheard of stretch of drafts and defensive coordinator Bud Carson's "Steel Curtain" defense coming into its own, Noll turned things around slowly. Of course, he didn't make a lot of friends with his players. He just showed them how to win.

"It wasn't his job to motivate people. His job was to teach and make us better, and that's what he did," Bleier said. "Chuck was a good leader, but he wasn't a rah-rah guy. He wasn't a player's coach. He'd say his door was always open but no one ever walked through it. But he had a great sense of treating people the way they needed to be treated. He wasn't checking rules but if you weren't performing and putting out in practice, you might be out of there. He gave everyone enough rope to hang themselves."

"Chuck is not going to win the most congeniality or most personable contest," said Dwight White, whom the Steelers picked in the fourth round of the 1971 draft. "But that's not what the business is—it's not a popularity contest. I think Chuck did an excellent job of keeping all those personalities in line. You almost need a psychology guy, a heady guy like Chuck to play the head games with these people.... You need some way to get into their heads and make them all be focused and channel all that energy in the right direction to win football games. We had some characters, but Chuck was able to find that middle ground and keep everybody content.

"The talent spoke for itself.... We were ready to go. We'd play

Bud Carson talks with defensive back Mike Wagner during a 1975 game at Three Rivers Stadium.

every day if you wanted to play every day. We could play a game every day. It was that type of attitude. As far as motivating people, Chuck didn't have to do that. That was not the issue. Keeping everybody focused was the issue. And he did a good job with that."

There is no way to put a value on what Chuck Noll brought to the Steeler organization during his 23-year reign. Almost single-handedly, he turned a perennial loser into one of the greatest dynasties in pro football history.

When he retired after the 1991 season, his teams had won 209 games, went to the playoffs 12 times, and reached the conference championship game seven times. He was elected to the Pro Football Hall of Fame in 1993, his first year of eligibility.

DID YOU KNOW...

The man generally credited with being the "father" of Dallas's famed "Doomsday Defense" is Pittsburgh Steelers great Ernie Stautner? Stautner, who coached at several places—including Pittsburgh—after a 14-year playing career with the Steelers that included having his No. 70 retired, was the Cowboys' defensive coordinator under Tom Landry.

BUD CARSON: ARCHITECT OF THE STEEL CURTAIN

Although Chuck Noll deserves much of the credit for the Steelers defense of the 1970s, one man who shouldn't be overlooked is Bud Carson.

Carson, who joined the Steelers as defensive coordinator in 1972, is generally regarded as the architect of the famed Steel Curtain defense. He's also an afterthought compared to Noll and the defensive players who dominated teams in the 1970s.

"He's very underrated," linebacker Andy Russell said without hesitating. "But I'd say he was a genius. He did things that were unheard of."

Carson's main innovation was a stunt 4–3 and double zone defense. At the time, playing a zone defense in the secondary was unheard of. So teams really didn't know how to throw against it. With the stunt 4–3 up front, teams had a difficult time running the ball.

It also didn't hurt to have defensive players who could audible based on the offense. Instead of just lining up and putting your regular defense against whatever the offense was doing, which was how things were done usually, Carson wanted to outsmart the offense.

"I had an interesting conversation with Bill Walsh one time," remembered Russell. "He had been the assistant offensive coordinator with Cincinnati. Walsh liked to come out in multiple sets. Bud Carson, all week long, couldn't decide what defense to do.

NFL'S FEWEST RUSHING YARDS ALLOWED IN A SEASON

1. Chicago Bears, 1942, 519 yards
2. Philadelphia, 1944, 558 yards
3. Pittsburgh, 1982, 762 yards (9-game season)

Obviously the defense wants to run the best defense to stop the opponent's best play in a particular offensive set. Carson didn't want to just stop the best play, he wanted to be in the best defense for each set. He wanted to move every time they moved. We'd change five times if they changed five times. As defensive players we were responsible to know if they changed."

"He gave us the defenses on Thursday or Friday. So much for learning everything in training camp. We were constantly memorizing. Before this Cincinnati game, we were in the tunnel about to be introduced before the game. Carson came running down and said, 'I've been up all night and I've changed all the defenses. Instead of doing this, we're going to do this.' We changed the whole thing and we played the checks he had just given us. He started worrying that Walsh was figuring out what we're doing. So he grabbed us when we came off the field one time in the second quarter and said, 'Okay, every other sequence we'll go back to Friday and then to Sunday.' Bill Walsh didn't believe that story. But it was true."

> **TRIVIA**
>
> Name the six teams that never won at Three Rivers Stadium.
>
> Find the answers on pages 165–166.

Carson was the Steelers' defensive coordinator through the 1977 season. He then went to the Los Angeles Rams in the same capacity. While there, the Rams lost to the Steelers in Super Bowl XIV.

Carson was the head coach at Cleveland for less than two seasons, compiling a 11–13–1 record in 1989–90.

Even though people want to point to Carson's stint with the

A LESSON IN TOUGHNESS

There might not be a better story to demonstrate the toughness of the Steel Curtain. There's certainly not a better one to display Dwight "Mad Dog" White's tenacity. It happened before the team's first Super Bowl, IX in New Orleans, in January 1975.

The Sunday night the Steelers arrived in New Orleans for the next week's game, Joe Greene, L.C. Greenwood, and White thought they'd grab some seafood and take in the atmosphere of the French Quarter. After dinner White started feeling sick. He was admitted to the hospital later that night with pleurisy and viral pneumonia.

Sicker than...well, a dog, he stayed there until Thursday, three days before the big game. He was so sick that he lost nearly 20 pounds during that brief stay. Not really ideal for an athlete who's wanting to be in tip-top shape for the biggest game of his life and also of his team's 40-year existence.

"But I couldn't miss the big dance; it was my lifetime dream," White said. "Being sick for the Super Bowl is totally unacceptable."

So White willed himself out of the hospital and onto the turf at Tulane Stadium. And through sheer determination, White played in each Pittsburgh defensive series except the last one.

What's more, White gave the Steelers their first-ever points in a Super Bowl game when he sacked Minnesota quarterback Fran Tarkenton in the end zone for a safety.

The Steelers drafted White out of East Texas State in the fourth round of the 1971 draft, which is the same one that included Jack Ham, Larry Brown, and Ernie Holmes.

For 10 seasons, 1971–80, White was a tenacious member of the Steel Curtain.

Browns as an indication of the job he could do when he had the right players—as he did in Pittsburgh—it was clear he could do exactly what he needed to do to be successful. And the players, feeding off that, were prepared and ready.

"While many of today's athletes have to consult horoscopes before they play, on Sunday I was always ready to kick some ass,"

Joe Greene, the anchor of the Steel Curtain, said in 1995. "I wasn't worried about being penalized for cut blocks or head slaps; I'd get after a guy. When the Steelers were playing, it was like Jaws was in the water. Everyone else had to get the hell out of there."

"I don't think the National Football League has seen a better defense than Pittsburgh's Steel Curtain," said former Dallas quarterback Roger Staubach, who lost against that defense in Super Bowls X and XIII. "We weren't the type of offense that they liked to play against because we tried to finesse them. They liked it when opponents tried to go head-to-head with them so they could beat the tar out of that team. They were very physical. We tried to trick them and they didn't like that. Unfortunately we didn't trick them enough."

In December 2005, Bud Carson died at his home in Florida after being ill with emphysema. He was 75.

BILL COWHER: EX-BROWN COMES HOME

It's hard to believe Bill Cowher was a Cleveland Brown—or at least hard to believe that an ex-Brown could do so many great things for the Steelers and be so beloved in Pittsburgh.

When Chuck Noll retired as head coach after the 1991 season, the Steelers were in a situation they hadn't faced since 1969: finding a new main man. That search took them to Kansas City, where former Cleveland Browns player Bill Cowher was the defensive coordinator. Of course, Bill Cowher was a Pittsburgh guy, from his work ethic, to his toughness, to his strong jaw, to his Carlynton High School diploma, circa 1975. He even used to attend Steelers games with his dad, Laird, who was a season-ticket holder back in the Forbes Field days.

Cleveland ties aside, the only true concern about Cowher was age and experience. He was green. Shoot, he was only 34, just four months older than Steelers offensive tackle Tunch Ilkin. His coaching resume was simple: seven seasons as an assistant, all under Marty Schottenheimer.

"I don't think when you're hiring a head coach if you know if they're ready till you give him the opportunity," Schottenheimer said. "(Cowher is) an extremely bright, hard-working individual. He's a good teacher, very demanding. Really, the thing that needs to happen, the only way to see how far he can go, is to do it."

They did. After an exhaustive search, the Steelers hired Cowher on January 21, 1992, mainly over then-Dallas defensive coordinator (and Pitt graduate) Dave Wannstedt.

Despite complacency—i.e., one trip to the playoffs from 1985 to 1991 during Noll's final few seasons, right off the bat in 1992, the Steelers apparently had the right man for the job. Pittsburgh won its first three games—two of which were on the road. The team finished with an 11–5 record and its first AFC Central Division championship in eight years.

The Buffalo Bills, that year's eventual AFC champ, beat the Steelers in the divisional playoffs, 24–3, but Cowher had laid the template for the Steelers' future success: a tough, hard-nosed team with a fierce defense. They quickly learned and improved from that first playoff experience.

After an overtime loss at Kansas City in a 1993 wild-card playoff game, the Steelers went 12–4 in 1994 before eventually losing the heartbreaker to San Diego in the AFC Championship Game. Then, in 1995, Cowher's fourth season, it all came together with a trip to Super Bowl XXX.

The only blemish on Cowher's record in Pittsburgh was a three-year dry spell, 1998–2000, when the Steelers missed the playoffs each year and finished under .500 twice. (Sadly, that coincided with the last three years of Three Rivers Stadium's existence.) Following the 6–10 campaign of 1999, which included a loss to the expansion Cleveland Browns, Cowher offered his resignation, including letting the team out of the final year of his guaranteed contract. The Rooneys wouldn't hear of it.

"Whatever's in the best interests of the Pittsburgh Steelers is what I wanted the decision to be made for," Cowher told the *Pittsburgh Post-Gazette* before the 2000 season. "I did not want to be head coach of this football team than for any other reason than I was the right guy. As long as Mr. Rooney felt that way, I was glad to be allowed to stay. I like this job. I've been very blessed."

It took a few years, but as he did when the Rooney family and the Steelers took a chance on him as a rookie head coach in 1992, Cowher rewarded Steelers Nation. From 2001 to 2005, the Steelers reached the AFC Championship Game three times. Of course it culminated with Cowher's crowning moment—the organization's elusive "one for the thumb"—a victory in Super Bowl XL.

"The team of the 1970s put Pittsburgh on the map," Cowher said in his press conference the day after the Steelers beat Seattle in Detroit. "They created a tradition and legacy. We're proud of that tradition, and for us to say that we kind of did that, too, in 2005, well, it was neat to be a little part of that tradition this year."

Immediately, though, the question quietly began circulating. Would he ride off into the sunset with his dream Super Bowl title like his star running back, Jerome Bettis? After all, Cowher and his wife, Kaye, had bought a house in Raleigh, North Carolina. Their two oldest daughters, Meagan and Lauren, were playing basketball collegiately for Princeton. Their youngest daughter, Lindsey, also a basketball player, was in high school.

Besides, family had always been important to Cowher. Whether to help stay grounded and focused on his family, or just to not take his work home with him, Cowher enforced a rule in his household that, win or lose, a player or a coach had 24 hours to sulk or celebrate. After that, it was on with life. While Meagan and Lauren were at Princeton, Cowher loved sending cookies to the girls each week. He set aside time from his hectic coaching schedule each week to have phone conversations with each girl.

Even though Cowher coached one more season, an 8–8 finish, his heart was with his family. "I'm not burned out," Cowher said during his resignation press conference. "There comes a time in your life—I'm healthy and happy, and I've been fortunate—you've got to prioritize things. My family has made a lot of sacrifices for me, and I'm looking forward to being there for them. It's the right time."

During Cowher's 15 years with the Steelers, which included eight division championships and a 161–99–1 record, 105 head coaches were hired in the NFL.

**Bill Cowher proudly hoists the Vince Lombardi Trophy after the Steelers'
21–10 win in Super Bowl XL over the Seattle Seahawks on February 5, 2006.**

Cowher spent the 2007 season as a studio analyst for CBS Sports' coverage of the NFL. The assumption is that he'll return to coaching one day, possibly sooner rather than later. Even if he returned as the head coach of the Browns (gulp), Bill Cowher will remain one of the most beloved Steelers in the team's history. Okay, maybe not if he came back with the Browns, but there certainly wouldn't be any denying Bill Cowher's importance in Steelers history.

EQUAL OPPORTUNITY

RAY KEMP

Art Rooney didn't really care about the color of skin. He just wanted the best players on his team.

Ray Kemp didn't really care about playing football professionally. Oh, he was a good college player at Duquesne University, where he played for Elmer Layden, one of the legendary Notre Dame four horsemen and, later, the commissioner of the National Football League. But in 1932 Kemp was ready to pursue his law degree.

At the Duquesne athletic banquet, Rooney convinced Kemp to play for the J.P. Rooneys, a semipro team, while pursuing his graduate degree. Additionally, Kemp was an assistant coach for Layden and he also played for another semipro team, the Erie Pros.

Then, in 1933 Pennsylvania banished the "blue laws" that prohibited organized leagues to play on Sunday, and Rooney entered the National Football League with the Pittsburgh Pirates. Rooney invited Kemp to play with them.

Kemp joining the Pirates wasn't seen the same way as Jackie Robinson signing with baseball's Dodgers. After all, 12 African Americans had played in the NFL from its inception in 1920 until the Pirates joined the league. However, only one, Joe Lillard of the Chicago Cardinals, was currently playing when Kemp and the Pirates began play in the NFL.

But Kemp was going to be a pioneer and would still have to

put up with the verbal and physical abuse that would accompany his trailblazing efforts.

Much like Robinson, who broke baseball's color barrier in 1947, Kemp had the perfect demeanor for any abuse he would take as racial tension in the United States grew in 1933, the worst year of the Depression. At that time, the unemployment rate was at approximately 25 percent with the national income at half of what it was at the start of the Depression four years earlier.

Kemp was tough and even-keeled. For nearly a year after graduating from Cecil High School, Kemp worked in the coal mines.

"I was going to come out to be the baddest football player in the county," Kemp said in 1998.

Fate stepped in and forced Kemp back onto the field. Maybe before he thought of himself as the "baddest football player." While working in the mine, Kemp's right foot was smashed by a slab of rock. His doctor, who happened to be his high school football coach, convinced Kemp that a smashed foot might not be the worst thing that could happen in the mines to Kemp and his future college football career.

So Kemp enrolled at Duquesne and tried out for football. Originally, he was one of three black players on the team. After his first year, the other two quit.

"I can't remember even playing against another black player the whole four years I played at Duquesne," said Kemp, who was an honorable mention selection for the All-American team as a tackle during his senior year.

After a year of playing—again as the only African American—with the J.P. Rooneys and the Erie Pros, along with his graduate studies and assistant coaching duties at Duquesne, Kemp joined the first-year Pirates in 1933.

Kemp's numbers with the Pirates aren't that impressive. Really, he played in only four games for the team. It certainly wasn't his fault.

In the team's first game, a 23–2 loss to the defending Eastern Division champion New York Giants, Kemp nearly recorded an interception.

"I had my hands taped heavily because that's what we did in

those days for linemen," Kemp said. "On about the third or fourth play I was in, I broke through and their passer threw the ball right into my hands, but I couldn't hold it because of the tape."

The next week, the Pirates faced the Chicago Cardinals, which featured the league's other African American player, running back Joe Lillard, whose quickness oftentimes made defenders tackle air initially. Lillard was having such a good game against the Pirates that player-coach Jap Douds was incensed at halftime.

"Listen, we got to get that nigger out of that damn game," Douds screamed. "He's just running all over you. Are you afraid of that nigger?"

When the Pirates left the locker room, Douds, who just happened to play tackle like Kemp, apologized to Kemp.

"You know, Ray, I didn't mean you."

During the fourth quarter, Lillard was ejected for fighting and the Pirates came back and won 14–13. It was the team's first win in the NFL.

After Pittsburgh's third game, a 21–6 loss to the Boston Redskins, Douds sent Kemp a letter stating that he was being cut from the team. Kemp tried to talk with Art Rooney about it, but to no avail.

Rooney said to Kemp, "Ray, I feel you are as good a ballplayer as we have on the club, but I am not going over the head of the coach."

About two months later, on December 1, Kemp was invited back to play in the final game of the 1933 season at New York. It didn't come without a price. Even in New York Kemp was turned away at the team hotel. He ended up staying at the Harlem YMCA.

Against the Giants that week, Kemp played the entire game. It was the last one he'd play in the NFL.

Kemp never put that law degree to use. After his playing career, he went on to a successful career as an educator and varsity football, basketball, and track and field coach at Bluefield State College in West Virginia, Lincoln University in Missouri, and Tennessee State University, where he was also the athletic director.

He became a member of the Duquesne University Sports Hall of Fame, the Western Pennsylvania Sports Hall of Fame, and he was recognized as one of football's black pioneers by the Pro Football Hall of Fame.

On March 26, 2002, Ray Kemp died at the age of 94 in Ashtabula, Ohio. He was the last surviving member of the original Pittsburgh Steelers. Coincidentally, two days before Kemp died, Denzel Washington and Halle Berry became just the second and third African Americans to win an Academy Award for best actor and actress, respectively. Berry was the first black woman to win the award.

In spite of Kemp's small statistical accomplishments on the field, his legacy not only with the Steelers' organization but also with the National Football League is as strong as any player ever to play in Pittsburgh.

"I didn't know him, obviously, as a player," Dan Rooney told the *Pittsburgh Post-Gazette* upon Kemp's death, "but when he came back in the '40s and '50s, he would always make a fuss over us all. He was very proud of being a Steeler."

LOWELL PERRY LEADS THE WAY

It would be easy to make Lowell Perry a sidebar or footnote in the history of the Pittsburgh Steelers. After all, his NFL playing career lasted all of six games in 1956 before a hip injury ended it.

Perry was injured when he took a handoff on a reverse and was hammered by the New York Giants' Rosey Grier, who hit Perry with such power that it fractured his pelvis and dislocated his hip.

Perry was in the hospital for 13 weeks. While there, Art Rooney visited Perry daily and made him a promise. "Lowell," the Chief said, "as long as I own the Pittsburgh Steelers, you have a job in my organization."

True to his word, Rooney and the Steelers made Perry the NFL's first African American assistant coach the next year. He also was the league's first black coach since World War II. Perry spent one year in that capacity.

Lowell Perry, a star football player at Michigan in the 1950s who played just six games for the Steelers, became the first black coach in the NFL after World War II.

DID YOU KNOW...

After Ray Kemp, the Steelers didn't have another black player until 1952 when they drafted Jack Spinks, an offensive lineman and fullback, out of Alcorn State (then Alcorn A&M)? Spinks played in only 10 games for the Steelers, which included 94 rushing yards on 22 carries and 22 receiving yards. Although Spinks played five seasons in the NFL with four teams, his best season was his rookie campaign with Pittsburgh. Since 1992, Alcorn State has played its home games at Jack Spinks Stadium in Lorman, Mississippi.

So, on the surface, it would be easy to end Lowell Perry's story there.

But after Perry left the Steelers, he went back to his home state of Michigan and finished his degree—which he had started at Duquesne University Law School—at the Detroit College of Law.

Perry became an attorney with the National Labor Relations Board, and then went to work for Chrysler as a labor relations lawyer in 1963. He was one of the lead people for Chrysler in a contract negotiation with the United Auto Workers in 1971.

He also managed Chrysler plants in Michigan.

President Gerald Ford picked Perry in May 1975 to head the Equal Employment Opportunity Commission, which Perry did for a year.

Later, years after retiring from Chrysler, Perry took over Michigan's labor department and Office of Urban Programs.

Along the way, Perry, who was an outstanding receiver from the University of Michigan, also became the first African American NFL broadcaster when he was teamed with Joe Tucker in 1966 as an analyst on a CBS broadcast of a Steelers game.

Perry, who publicly never complained about the way his football career or post football career turned out, still encountered his share of racism in the NFL. One time, the Steelers were going to play an exhibition game against Baltimore in Jacksonville, Florida.

AFRICAN AMERICAN FIRSTS IN PRO FOOTBALL

First player—Charles Follis, Shelby Athletic Club, 1904
First player to win individual league stats title—Marion Motley, Cleveland of the All-America Football Conference, 1946
First player drafted by an NFL club—George Taliaferro, Chicago Bears, 1949, but played with the AAFC Los Angeles Dons
First draftee to play in the NFL—Wally Triplett, Detroit Lions, 1949
First NFL quarterback —Willie Thrower, Chicago Bears, 1953
First starting quarterback in a Super Bowl—Doug Williams, Washington Redskins, Super Bowl XXII, 1988
First player elected to Pro Football Hall of Fame—Emlen Tunnell, New York Giants and Green Bay Packers, defensive back, elected 1967
First general manager—Ozzie Newsome, Baltimore Ravens, 2002
First head coach—Fritz Pollard, Akron, 1921
First head coach in modern era (post–World War II)—Art Shell, Los Angeles Raiders, 1989
First assistant coach—Lowell Perry, Pittsburgh, 1957
First head coach to take team to, and win, Super Bowl—Tony Dungy, Indianapolis Colts, 2006 (won); Lovie Smith, Chicago Bears, 2006

The city was even going to have a parade for the teams.

The only problem was that the hotel where the Steelers were staying would not allow Perry and the team's black players to stay at the same hotel. He found that out on the flight to Florida. So when the plane landed, Perry grabbed the black players and took them directly to their hotel and avoided the parade.

"Later that day we were practicing at the Gator Bowl," Perry said, "and Art Rooney, who had come on a later plane, told all of the black players, 'I promise you, this will never happen to one of my teams again.'"

And, much like the hospital room promise Rooney had made to Perry, he held true to this one too. The next year, the Steelers were scheduled to play an exhibition game in Atlanta. Rooney caught wind that his black players would have to stay in a hotel away from the rest of his team. So Rooney canceled the game.

In 2000, Perry was diagnosed with cancer. He lost the battle in January 2001. He was 69.

Frankly, for whatever reason, once Ray Kemp and Joe Lillard were out of the league following the 1933 season, it would be 13 years before another African American played for any team in the NFL. The team owners swore there weren't any rules—unwritten or otherwise—against black players. It's just the way it worked out, they'd say. In 1946, a year before Jackie Robinson broke baseball's color barrier, the Los Angeles Rams signed Woody Strode and Kenny Washington.

HEROES ON AND OFF THE GRIDIRON

"BULLET" BILL DUDLEY: PITTSBURGH'S FIRST HERO

Bill Dudley was football's anomaly. He was slow and not particularly big at 5'10" and 182 pounds. But somehow he could play on both sides of the ball.

"He doesn't seem to be able to do anything real well, but he's a helluva football player," said fellow Hall of Famer Sammy Baugh. "I'd say Bill was a real specialist—specializing in everything."

The Steelers took Dudley in the first round of the 1942 NFL draft out of Virginia. To Baugh's point, Dudley played halfback, quarterback, defensive back, kicker, and punter.

Dudley, the team's first star, finally gave Pittsburgh fans a reason to cheer. In the 1942 season opener against Philadelphia, Dudley scooted 44 yards for a touchdown. The Steelers wasted the touchdown in a 24–14 loss.

In the second game of the season, Dudley hurt his ankle so badly during the first half that he had to be carried off the field. But he returned in the second half and ran the opening kickoff back for a Pittsburgh touchdown. Again, the Steelers wasted Dudley's electrifying effort with a 28–14 loss at Washington.

As a rookie, Dudley led the league in rushing with 696 yards on 162 carries. But Dudley had a strong desire to serve the United States in World War II. He actually wanted to become a navy pilot after college, but his parents wouldn't sign the consent form. So he played for the Steelers.

Getty Images

Bill Dudley takes off upfield during a September 1946 game against the Washington Redskins that ended in a 14–14 tie.

During the season, with America's efforts in the war intensifying, Dudley enlisted in the Army Air Corps. Because of the large number of recruits, Dudley had to wait three months before reporting for duty. He was able to finish his rookie season, which garnered him the Rookie of the Year award.

Dudley attended the army's flight school in Florida, but he didn't do much flying. He was asked to play for the army's football team as a "morale booster."

Finally, with four games remaining in the 1945 season, Dudley returned to the Steelers. Whether it's a testament to his ability or the team's futility, in those four games Dudley became the team's leading scorer with 20 points.

In 1946, Dudley became the first and only player to lead the league in four categories: rushing (604 yards), punt returns (14.3-yard average), interceptions (10), and lateral passing.

Art Rooney called Dudley the "best all-around football player I've ever seen."

"Dudley was a Jimmy Brown on offense and a 'Night Train' Lane on defense," Rooney added. "Steve Owens of the Giants and Greasy Neale of the Eagles imposed an automatic fine on their quarterbacks if they called a pass play into Dudley's territory."

Earlier that season, Jock Sutherland and his single-wing offense took over as Pittsburgh's head coach. Sutherland, who had his dentistry degree, for some reason didn't see eye to eye with Dudley. The ongoing feud left Dudley requesting a trade.

He got it the next season, being sent to Detroit in exchange for a first-round pick in 1948.

"I thoroughly enjoyed my time in Pittsburgh," said Dudley. "I'm sorry I couldn't have continued my whole career there. We played a good football game, got some good crowds in Pittsburgh, and I think the football we played kept the fans happy, both in '42 and '46."

The year Dudley was traded, 1947, happened to be the same year that the Steelers made it to the playoffs for the first time.

Dudley spent six seasons with Detroit and Washington before retiring after the 1953 season to work as an assistant coach at Virginia. He came back to Pittsburgh in 1956 to serve as assistant under Walt Kiesling.

"I'm very, very fond of Pittsburgh," Dudley said. "It's where I like to be remembered as playing ball. Nothing against Washington or Detroit, it was just my first stop, and I became friends with Mr. Rooney. He was an employer who later turned into a very good friend."

ROCKY BLEIER: GETTING A SECOND CHANCE

"As long as you keep moving forward, you'll reach the finish line."
—*Unknown*

Throughout each person's life we encounter at least one individual—whether it's as basic as a casual acquaintance or as

The indomitable Rocky Bleier, shown here in a 1975 photo, was among the Steelers', and the NFL's, most beloved players.

personal as a friendship—who teaches us about living and makes us realize that we can do better. It's these people whose lives can intimidate writers, or at least give writers a mental hurdle while trying to relay the story in a perfect way.

Rocky Bleier, who is best known as a running back with the great Steelers teams of the 1970s, is one of those people. His story, while worth telling and retelling, is challenging.

It's tough to find one word to describe Bleier and his life. Oh, you could use courageous, inspiring, athletic, heroic, unwavering, horrific, determined, incredible, astonishing, remarkable, and tenacious. And so many more. You could also throw in Super Bowl champion and college national champion, but of course neither of those is just one word.

Indeed, there isn't *one* word in the English language to describe

Bleier. Ernest Hemingway, John Steinbeck, Pat Conroy, and even the *Merriam-Webster* folks would struggle finding one word to describe Bleier.

The remarkable aspect of Bleier's life is not what he accomplished on the field per se.

"Like many people, I probably peaked when I was nine years old, in a game against my neighbor when I scored 52 touchdowns on one afternoon," Bleier quipped, laughing "That was probably the biggest game of my life, and it's been downhill ever since."

Actually, Bleier, a native of Appleton, Wisconsin, played an important role on Notre Dame's 1966 national championship team under coach Ara Parseghian. But he wasn't given much chance of making it in the NFL, particularly because of his 5'11", 205-pound frame. The Steelers didn't gamble a lot when they drafted him in the 16th round of the 1968 draft.

However, shortly thereafter is where the story takes its most revealing turn.

In December 1968, with three games left in his rookie season, Bleier received an unwanted piece of mail before practice...his draft notice for the U.S. Army. With the United States near the height of the Vietnam War, Bleier loved his country, but, c'mon, how many 22-year-olds really wanted to go to war?

"I can't say that I was gung-ho about serving," he said. "I can't say that I wanted to or needed to serve our country in time of war. Like most others, I was just an average guy who got a draft notice. I'm sure my thought process wasn't much different than anybody else who got drafted, when you look at that [notice] and say, 'Aw, (insert your own profanity)! How did I screw up? Now what do I do?' But you do what you think is right. You go and you serve."

When someone received a draft notice, he usually had a week before he had to report. Bleier's draft notice reached him late. He had one day to report. The Steelers tried to help him defer until the end of the season, but the best they could do was designate him with high blood pressure, giving him an extra day before reporting.

Five months later, in May 1969, Bleier was sent to Chu Lai, South Vietnam, with the 196th American Division's Light Infantry Brigade.

A few months later, in August, Bleier's life was altered in Heip Duc

TRIVIA

How many members of the team made it from Chuck Noll's arrival in 1969 through Super Bowl IX, the organization's first?

Find the answers on pages 165–166.

as he was crippled by enemy rifle fire and grenade wounds in both legs.

It appeared as though his NFL career—not to mention his ability to even walk normally—was finished. But while he was still in the army, Bleier worked to become a better football player.

"Whether it was by design or by the grace of God, or the lessons that I needed to learn, I fell through the cracks and came back alive," he says. "I went over there, I served, I got wounded, and I got wounded again. I wasn't wounded enough to not play, but enough to learn a lesson.

"People have asked me if the experience made me a better ballplayer. I would have to say yes, it did. If I hadn't gone, would I have been a better ballplayer? I don't know. I do know that what I wanted to do was come back from Vietnam and play football. That drove me. So I pushed myself.

"When I was in the service, I got up at 5:30 in the morning and ran prior to going to my duty station. When I got done with my duty, I came back and lifted weights. When I got done with that, I went home and ran sprints. All of that was part of wanting to come back with a focus."

Bleier, who was awarded a Purple Heart, a Bronze Star, and two campaign ribbons, came back with that same desire to play football. Steelers' owner Art Rooney, whether out of a belief in Bleier or pity for him, gave Bleier a second chance.

Bleier spent the 1970 season on injured reserve, but he continued to work out. The next year he made the taxi squad, and continued to work out in hopes of becoming a better player. Finally, in 1972, Bleier made the team's active roster.

"I think all of us want hope. As long as we can see the light at the end of the tunnel, we're okay," he said. "As long as there is hope, or a ray of hope, of either making the team or doing something that you love, then you push yourself forward."

Bleier became an important part of those championship

Steelers teams of the '70s. His best statistical season in 12 years with the Steelers came in 1976, when he rushed 220 times for 1,036 yards and five touchdowns, and caught 24 passes for 294 yards. He was best known on the field, however, as a great blocking back for Franco Harris, en route to four Super Bowl titles.

Bleier's best Super Bowl performance was in XIII, a 35–31 win over the Dallas Cowboys, when he caught a Terry Bradshaw pass for a touchdown and later snuffed out Dallas's onside kick attempt, preserving the championship.

Regardless of whether he was battling to run again, trying to help his team win a preseason game, or helping them win a Super Bowl title, Bleier was prepared to take advantage of the challenges and breaks in front of him, all the while striving to become better. His attitude is something most of us could use.

"The little things in our lives, all of a sudden, for some reason measure up to something else. Opportunities exist but you've got to be prepared and have a mind-set to push forward," he said. "Every year is a renewal. A renewal of hope, of a second chance, of starting over.

"We can look at the past, and what's been accomplished, but we can't live back there. A lot of people do; a lot of players do. Many times that causes their future to be determined by their past. Each year, hopefully, you learn about something and you get a second chance to do better. You get to renew, take an initiative, and move forward. In my life, on and off the field, I've been given second chances."

Bleier certainly applies those ideas to his own life. Besides receiving a second chance in football, he says he got a second opportunity in his personal life. After going through a tough divorce at the age of 50, Bleier remarried, and at the age of 55, he and his new wife adopted two infant girls from the Ukraine.

"I was given a second chance to do it over again, and better than I did in the past," said Bleier, who retired from football after the 1980 season. "We have to look at those situations and, instead of wondering why this or that happened, learn something from each of them and move on."

After his playing career, Bleier became a sought-after motivational speaker, although he says he's more of an inspirational

BYRON "WHIZZER" WHITE

How does one become a Supreme Court justice? Evidently by playing for the Pittsburgh Steelers. At least that's the route Byron "Whizzer" White took.

White, whom the Steelers drafted first in 1938, was up for the Heisman Trophy and led the nation in scoring and rushing at the University of Colorado. He was a statement signing for Art Rooney and the young Pirates organization. Rooney, whose teams hadn't finished better than 6–6 in their first five years, was looking for a boost. So he signed White for $15,800, which, in 1938, was an incredible amount, more than three times what the other NFL players were making. It made White the highest-paid professional athlete.

"The other owners were furious," said Dan Rooney. "[Washington owner] George Preston Marshall accosted Dad, saying, 'What are you trying to do, ruin the league?' But as I said, Dad was desperate. His losing team was not only losing fans, it was losing money. He thought the Whizzer could turn the team around, but although his new star impressed fans and opponents, even he couldn't overcome the erratic coaching and general poor play of the Pittsburgh team.... Byron White was a gentleman, scholar, and one of the greatest athletes I've ever seen."

White didn't disappoint on the field. He led the NFL in rushing with 567 yards. He also scored a team-leading four touchdowns. After that one season, though, White had had enough. After all, he had bigger things ahead.

White went to Oxford in 1939 as a Rhodes Scholar. He returned to play two seasons for Detroit. During World War II, White, as a naval intelligence officer, met John F. Kennedy when he wrote the official report on the sinking of Kennedy's boat, the PT-109. In 1962, Kennedy, then president, appointed White to the U.S. Supreme Court. He was a member of the nation's top court for 31 years.

speaker. While talking to an older gentleman on an airplane several years ago, Bleier learned a valuable lesson about motivation: people generally are motivated by one of two factors—love and fear. It's a concept that Bleier started using in his speeches.

"Ultimately, as much as we live in a world of change, we don't change. We won't really change until we have one of those two factors," said Bleier. "In my speeches I also talk about being the

NFL CAREER RUSHING TOUCHDOWN LEADERS

1. Emmitt Smith, 164
2. Marcus Allen, 123
3. LaDainian Tomlinson, 115
4. Walter Payton, 110
5. Jim Brown, 106
6. John Riggins, 104

7. Marshall Faulk, 100
8. Shaun Alexander, 100
9. Barry Sanders, 99
10. Jerome Bettis, 91
    Franco Harris, 91

best you can be. Sometimes that gets confused with living up to your potential. We all beat ourselves up because we don't feel like we're living up to our potential. Being the best is doing the best at whatever you're doing.

"You have to learn to appreciate who you are and what you're good at. We're not all good at everything. Don't beat yourself up because you're not good at something; just come to understand what your strengths and weaknesses are. Don't necessarily try to become better at something you hate to do. That gives you much more energy to do something you love to do, and that you're good at doing."

To think that, as with so many other American veterans, Bleier's life changed with one letter. In many ways, the lives of fans who followed Bleier's career changed with that letter.

"Vietnam is a part of my story and a part of who I am," he said. "Am I thankful for Vietnam? I'm thankful for the experience. I'm thankful for going. I'm thankful for having served. I'm thankful for the people I have served with, and those who served before and after me. I'm thankful for the people who know me and the relationship they have of one of those who defended our country."

Indeed, Rocky Bleier can give us a kick in the pants every now and then. He can teach us that we should be thankful for life's challenges. He can teach us about change and being our best and finding our strengths. He can teach us that we will reach the finish line with each new step. And he can teach us that we sometimes do get a second chance.

THROUGH THE DRAFT: GOOD AND BAD

Every team has its stories, the draft here and there that produces great players who stay with the organization for a Hall of Fame career. Each team also has huge busts, ones that make fans wish Morganna was playing instead of the deadwood the team drafted. The Steelers, however, have a few that coincide with the failures and successes of the organization.

OOPS! WHO SAW THIS ONE COMING?

The Steelers easily could've been the most celebrated championship team in the history of the NFL if they had kept at least one of three quarterbacks: Johnny Unitas, Len Dawson, or Jack Kemp. In terms of personnel moves, these rank among the three worst in franchise history. At one point during the 1950s, all three were Steelers. All three went on to great NFL careers after leaving Pittsburgh.

Johnny Unitas

The most celebrated and most obvious is Unitas, who set 22 NFL passing records, including 47 consecutive games with a touchdown pass. He was a three-time NFL Most Valuable Player and he won three NFL championships. The only problem is that he did all of that with the Baltimore Colts. Call it an unfair comparison, but he could've done it for the Steelers—he should've done it for the Steelers.

Throughout high school and college, coaches saw Unitas, a Pittsburgh kid from St. Justin's, as undersized. His height was

DID YOU KNOW...

A former executioner tried out for the Steelers in 1941? Well, actually, Big Arthur Jarrett—as he's referred in an Associated Press story from July 30, 1941—wasn't a full-blown executioner. He was only an assistant hangman at the penal colony on Oahu, Hawaii. As the story goes, Jarrett was a 23-year-old, 230-pound barefooted kicker when Steelers co-owner Bert Bell found out about him. Bizarre enough for you? If not, here you go. As far as the whole assistant hangman thing goes, Jarrett's dad was the warden of the penal colony, and Jarrett became a guard when he was old enough. According to the article, "As a sort of promotion, Jarrett was made assistant hangman. The grinning athlete admits he never actually served in an execution, largely because the regular hangman always was on the job."

Jarrett, a graduate of the University of Hawaii, was expected to end up at either guard or tackle for the Steelers. And, yes, he was expected to wear shoes.

"He was recommended to us by a former Pitt player," said Bell, who was in his first year as co-owner and general manager of the Steelers. "If he is half as good as his record indicates, he will be one of the regulars when the National [Football] League season gets under way."

Evidently Jarrett wasn't that good. He didn't make the squad.

---

respectable at six feet or so, but he was relatively skinny at about 170 pounds by the time he finished his collegiate career at the University of Louisville. (He weighed 138 at the end of his high school career when he tried to get noticed by his favorite college, Notre Dame.)

So, during the 1955 draft, most teams passed on him. And continued to pass on him. An unbelievable 101 players were chosen before him. Finally, in the ninth round, Dan Rooney, who had played against Unitas in high school and was helping manage the draft for the Steelers, urged Ray Byrne to draft Unitas. They did just that, much to the chagrin of head coach Walt Kiesling, who liked physical football. He wasn't a fan of Unitas's size, but more important, he thought Unitas was "too dumb to play."

Granted, the Steelers had three quarterbacks at the time—Jim Finks, Vic Eaton, and Ted Marchibroda. It might not have mattered

BY THE NUMBERS

6—The number of Steelers on the NFL's 75th Anniversary All-Time Team. They are: Mel Blount, Joe Greene, Jack Ham, Jack Lambert, Mike Webster, and Rod Woodson.

if the team had only one. Kiesling, who generally wouldn't budge from his personal beliefs, never gave Unitas a chance to play during training camp. Unitas resorted to throwing on the side to Art Rooney's sons, Tim, John, and Pat.

The Rooney boys saw how good Unitas was and tried to convince the Chief to intervene. Art Rooney, also a man of his convictions, wouldn't overrule his head coach, even when Tim wrote the Chief a 22-page letter about why the Steelers needed to keep Unitas.

"I like John too," Rooney said, "but Kies is the coach, let him do his job."

Kiesling cut Unitas at the end of camp. The following season he landed with the Baltimore Colts, where he became the legendary "Johnny U."

"The Unitas story stays with me as a reminder that sometimes you have to trust your instincts even if those around you, people you know and trust, don't agree," Dan Rooney wrote in his book, *Dan Rooney: My 75 Years with the Pittsburgh Steelers and the NFL*. "In this case, my brothers and I were right; Kies and Dad were wrong."

Unitas was elected to the Pro Football Hall of Fame in 1979.

Len Dawson

Len Dawson's collegiate career was better than Unitas's. And his prospects in the NFL were brighter. At Purdue, Dawson had thrown for more than 3,000 yards, led the Big Ten in passing for three seasons, and led the Boilermakers to an upset over top-ranked Notre Dame in South Bend. Before the draft, the Steelers and the Cleveland Browns were among the teams that contacted Dawson to see if he'd be interested in playing if they drafted him.

BY THE NUMBERS

Highest Passer Rating, Rookie Season, NFL History
98.1, Ben Roethlisberger, 2004
96.0, Dan Marino, 1983
88.2, Greg Cook, 1969

The Steelers beat the Browns in a coin flip to see which team would draft in front of the other. Of course, the Steelers picked Dawson. Kiesling was the coach at the time of the draft, but he resigned before the season because of health reasons. When training camp opened, Buddy Parker had taken over.

"Buddy was going to do it his way, and Buddy was known as a coach who didn't play rookies, particularly at quarterback," said Dawson. "I knew right away when they got another coach who hadn't drafted me that I wasn't going to play much."

Indeed, Dawson didn't. During his three years in Pittsburgh, Dawson played in just 19 games, starting in only one. He completed six of 17 passes for 96 yards and one touchdown. It was also during Dawson's Pittsburgh career that the Steelers signed Bobby Layne, Parker's old quarterback and friend in Detroit.

In December 1959, the Steelers traded Dawson to Cleveland, where he spent two benchwarming seasons before signing with the American Football League's Dallas Texans in 1962. The Texans, which moved to Kansas City in 1963 and became the Chiefs, flourished with Dawson. He led them to two AFL championships, and then to victory in Super Bowl IV over the Minnesota Vikings.

Dawson was elected to the Pro Football Hall of Fame in 1987.

Jack Kemp

Although he was selected out of Occidental by Detroit in the 17th round of the January 1957 NFL draft, Jack Kemp was another of Buddy Parker's guys.

So, even though Kemp was a rookie, shortly after Parker left

BY THE NUMBERS

Most Career Interceptions Returned for a Touchdown in NFL History

12, Rod Woodson
9, Ken Houston
9, Aeneas Williams
9, Deion Sanders
8, Eric Allen
8, Darren Sharper

Detroit and became the Steelers coach, he acquired Kemp as Bobby Layne's backup quarterback.

During the '57 season, Kemp threw for 88 yards and no touchdowns in four games. He also punted twice for 55 yards. That was the extent of Kemp's career in Pittsburgh. At training camp in 1958, Kemp disobeyed an order from Parker to punt a ball out of bounds. Kemp's punt was returned for a touchdown. As the story goes, Parker released Kemp immediately—during the game.

Kemp bounced around as a professional benchwarmer before Sid Gillman and the Los Angeles–San Diego Chargers signed him in 1960. In 1962, the Chargers tried to sneak him through the American Football League's waiver line. The Buffalo Bills, needing help at quarterback, snatched Kemp for the $100 fee.

Kemp went on to lead the Bills to AFL championships in 1964 and '65. In 1965 he was picked as the AFL's Player of the Year. Kemp retired after the 1969 season and became highly successful in both business and politics. He served in Congress for 18 years, followed by four years as the secretary of Housing and Urban Development.

Kemp's only failure, of sorts, was not being elected to the White House in 1988 and then another miss as the Republican Party's nomination for vice president, to run with Bob Dole in 1996.

BY THE NUMBERS

NFL Hall of Fame Players Drafted 1969–74

Yr. Drafted	Rd./Pick/Over.	Player	Team	Pos.	School	HOF
1969	1/1/1	O.J. Simpson	Bills	RB	USC	1985
1969	1/4/4	Joe Greene	Steelers	DT	N. Texas St.	1987
1969	2/7/33	Ted Hendricks	Colts	LB	Miami	1990
1969	4/15/93	Charlie Joiner	Oilers	WR	Grambling	1996
1969	1/19/19	Roger Wehrli	Cardinals	DB	Missouri	2007
1970	1/1/1	Terry Bradshaw	Steelers	QB	La. Tech	1989
1970	3/1/53	Mel Blount	Steelers	DB	Southern	1989
1971	1/6/6	John Riggins	Jets	RB	Kansas	1992
1971	1/20/20	Jack Youngblood	Rams	DE	Florida	2001
1971	2/8/34	Jack Ham	Steelers	LB	Penn State	1988
1971	2/17/43	Dan Dierdorf	Cardinals	T	Michigan	1996
1972	1/13/13	Franco Harris	Steelers	RB	Penn State	1990
1973	1/4/4	John Hannah	Patriots	G	Alabama	1991
1973	1/26/26	Joe De Lamielleure	Bills	G	Michigan St.	2003
1973	3/12/64	Dan Fouts	Chargers	QB	Oregon	1993
1974	1/21/21	Lynn Swann	Steelers	WR	USC	2001
1974	2/19/45	Dave Casper	Raiders	TE	Notre Dame	2002
1974	2/20/46	Jack Lambert	Steelers	LB	Kent State	1990
1974	4/4/82	John Stallworth	Steelers	WR	Ala. A&M	2002
1974	5/21/125	Mike Webster	Steelers	C	Wisconsin	1997

DRAFTING A DYNASTY

Each year, every team in the NFL goes into the draft hoping, expecting to find at least a few players who'll be able to contribute for years to come. There is no way, even in their wildest prayers, that any NFL executive could come close to equaling what the Steelers accomplished through the draft from 1969 through '74.

Chuck Noll, in his first head coaching gig, preferred building the team through the draft. He wanted young guys he could mold instead of retreads who either were no longer useful to their previous clubs or weren't good enough to succeed in other places. (Hence the hamster wheel that became the "Same Old Steelers.")

Starting with Noll's first year as head coach and the decision to go with a relatively unknown Joe Greene with the team's first pick in 1969 through the fifth-round selection of Mike Webster in 1974, the Steelers picked nine future Hall of Famers.

They also got several other players who were instrumental in building toward a dynasty: Terry Hanratty, Jon Kolb, L.C. Greenwood, Dwight White, Larry Brown, Ernie Holmes, and Joe Gilliam. Plus there was Donnie Shell, who signed undrafted.

The draft was so fruitful for the Steelers during that stretch that by the time the team played in its fourth Super Bowl, XIV against the Los Angeles Rams, not one member of the Pittsburgh team had played for another organization. And the incredible number of 22 players played on each of those first four Super Bowl teams.

Other organizations have had great drafts with multiple future Hall of Famers. The Green Bay Packers picked Ray Nitschke and Jim Taylor, plus great guard Jerry Kramer in 1958. The Kansas City Chiefs drafted Buck Buchanan and Bobby Bell in 1963. In 1965, the Chicago Bears selected Gale Sayers and Dick Butkus.

But no team has had a stretch like the Steelers had from 1969 to 1974.

SO CLOSE, BUT NO

In a perfect world, everyone learns from mistakes. That certainly didn't apply to the Steelers in the 1983 draft. After letting a quarterback from their own backyard—the great Johnny Unitas—go on to a Hall of Fame career with another team, the Steelers had a chance to pick another solid quarterback from Pennsylvania.

The 1983 draft was the year of the quarterback. Even without getting lucky with a guy from a smaller school such as Terry Bradshaw (from Louisiana Tech), there were plenty of solid college quarterbacks in the '83 NFL draft. John Elway, Todd Blackledge, Jim Kelly, Tony Eason, and Dan Marino all had been successful at what we now know as "BCS" schools. Big programs. Then there was Ken O'Brien, who had been a good player at the University of California at Davis.

In some fairness, the Steelers had who they thought would be Bradshaw's replacement in Mark Malone (1983 was Bradshaw's last season). And by the time the Steelers drafted 21st, Elway, Blackledge, Kelly, and Eason were gone.

However, in some fairness to common sense, Dan Marino, a Pennsylvania kid who had a great career at Pitt, would seem like a good pick.

The Steelers thought otherwise and went with defensive lineman Gabe Rivera out of Texas Tech. By no stretch was Rivera a bad player to choose. After all, he was the Southwest Conference's Defensive Player of the Year.

Six games into his NFL career, after recording two sacks, Rivera lost control of his car and crashed. He had been drinking and wasn't wearing his seat belt. The accident left him paralyzed from the chest down. In an instant, his football career was over.

The accident notwithstanding, some schools of thought say that if your quarterback situation is questionable, and one's available in the draft, you pick him. The Steelers went against that philosophy.

And, finally, Pittsburgh learned from that mistake. In 2004, with the 11th overall pick, the Steelers selected Ben Roethlisberger out of the University of Miami (Ohio). The decision to go with "Big Ben" was a direct result of bypassing Marino 21 years earlier.

"I couldn't bear the thought of passing on another great quarterback prospect the way we had passed on Dan Marino in 1983, so I steered the conversation [with scouts and Steelers staff] around to Roethlisberger," Dan Rooney wrote in his 2007 autobiography, *Dan Rooney: My 75 Years with the Pittsburgh Steelers and the NFL*. "After some more talk, we came to a consensus and picked Roethlisberger. Big Ben, six-foot-five, 240 pounds, was quick, tough, had a great arm, and could think on his feet. He was just what we needed."

BROWNS AND GIANTS AND RAIDERS, OH MY!

The Steelers have had great rivalries over the years. In fact, one of the sticking points in the formation of the AFC Central when the AFL and the NFL merged was that the Steelers had to keep their rivals. Namely, they didn't want to lose the Cleveland Browns. At the same time, they picked up the Cincinnati Bengals.

Although the Steelers and Bengals aren't really fans of one another, the rivalry hasn't had the same type of ferocity or importance that the rivalries with the Browns and the Oakland Raiders have had throughout the years. In fact, when one team dominates the other, as the Steelers have done with the Bengals, is it still a rivalry?

The following stories celebrate three rivalries: the inter-conference rivalry with the Browns, the longtime NFC (or NFL if you're old-school) foe in the Giants, and a championship-caliber rivalry with the Raiders.

THE BROWNS

Unlike many rivalries, when the underdog oftentimes wins simply because it's a rivalry, the Steelers-Browns series has been marked by winning (or losing) streaks.

It started immediately. When Cleveland came into the league in 1950, the Browns won 16 of the first 18 games in the series. Then, from 1962–70, still the "Same Old Steelers" years, the Browns took 14 of those 17 games. After splitting the four games

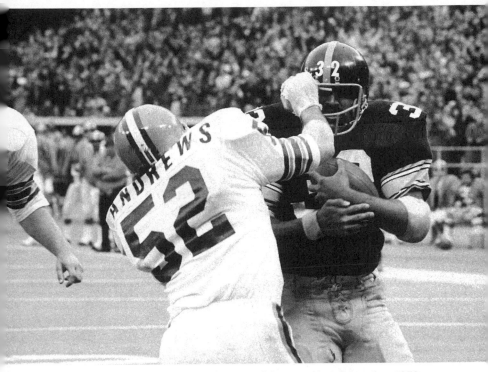

Franco Harris attempts to smash through for a score in a December 1972 game against the Cleveland Browns. The ferocity of the Steelers' rivalry with the Browns dates back to the early 1950s.

in 1970 and '71, the Steelers went 16–4 against the Browns over their next 20 games. The Steelers' domination continues. Since 2000, Pittsburgh has won 15 of 17 games.

In spite of the crazy streaks for the two teams, heading into the 2007 season they were dead even in the series, 55–55. The Steelers won both contests in '07, giving them a two-game advantage.

Although relatively meaningless in the grand scheme of things, one game that stands out is the September 24, 1978, meeting in Pittsburgh. Both teams went into the game unde-feated. Both offenses struggled to get the ball across the goal line. Cleveland took a 9–3 lead in the third quarter with all of the game's points coming on field goals. The Steelers put together back-to-back drives in the fourth quarter that resulted in two field

BY THE NUMBERS

16—The number of consecutive home victories over the Cleveland Browns (1970–1985).

23—The number of wins over the Browns at Three Rivers Stadium.

goals and the game was headed to overtime.

In overtime, after a controversial no-fumble call when Pittsburgh's Larry Anderson appeared to have lost the ball, the Steelers were on the Cleveland 37. Terry Bradshaw handed off to Rocky Bleier, who handed the ball to Lynn Swann. Instead of taking it on the reverse, Swann tossed the ball back to Bradshaw, who threw a long touchdown pass to Bennie Cunningham. It happened to be Bradshaw's 100th career touchdown pass, in addition to the game winner.

The Steelers and Browns didn't meet for three seasons, 1996–98, because, well, Cleveland didn't have a team. That's when Art Modell decided to move to Baltimore. It was nice when Cleveland got the new version of the Browns before the 1999 season because it was a chance for the Steelers to restart their domination. And they did.

In the Browns' return game, a Sunday night affair in '99 in Cleveland, Kordell Stewart accounted for 208 yards (173 yards passing, 35 rushing), and the Pittsburgh defense held Cleveland to nine yards rushing in a crushing 43–0 win. It's the largest margin of victory for Pittsburgh in this series.

Surprisingly, during their 112-game history the Steelers and the Browns have played each other only twice during the postseason. One of those games, though, provided one of the most exciting, most stunning games in the rivalry.

It happened on January 5, 2003. During the regular season, the Steelers had defeated Cleveland twice, a 16–13 overtime win at Heinz Field and a 23–20 victory in Cleveland.

During 2002, the Steelers proved more than a couple times that they didn't have a typical Pittsburgh defense. The 2002 version gave up points. A lot of them.

That trend continued when the Browns visited Heinz Field for the AFC wild-card game.

Cleveland backup quarterback Kelly Holcomb threw for 429 yards and three touchdowns. That's not to take anything away from Tommy Maddox, who threw for a Steeler playoff record 367 yards, three touchdowns, and two interceptions.

Late in the game, about five minutes into the fourth quarter, the Browns were up by 12 points, 33–21. Then, with 3:06 left in the game, after marching down the field with the no-huddle offense, Maddox and Hines Ward hooked up for a five-yard touchdown play, 33–28.

The Browns gave up the ball quickly on a three-and-out. The Steelers, fresh off a touchdown, got the ball on their own 39-yard line with 2:38 remaining.

Maddox went right to work with a 24-yard pass to Plaxico Burress. Then, after an incompletion, he completed passes to Ward, Burress, and Ward again. Suddenly, Maddox looked like the second coming of Terry Bradshaw (rather than a quarterback who became an insurance salesman, then an XFL signal caller, and then came back to the NFL). The Steelers used their final timeout with less than a minute left and the ball on the Cleveland 3-yard line.

The call went to Chris Fuamatu-Ma'afala, who ran to the right, found a hole, and barreled into the end zone for the game-winning touchdown with less than a minute to play.

"I don't think anybody in here's been part of a game where it ended like this," said Hines Ward. "I can't even describe the feeling right now. I've never in my whole life been part of a game like this."

"I'll tell you this, they'll be home next week," said Browns cornerback Corey Fuller. "They got one more week. We gave it to them today. Unbelievable."

Incidentally, the Tennessee Titans did beat the Steelers the next week, 34–31.

BY THE NUMBERS

30—The number of points scored in the Steelers' first shutout of the Cleveland Browns on December 3, 1972.

THE GIANTS

Much like the rivalry with the Bengals, where the Steelers have dominated the series, the New York Giants haven't had many problems with the Steelers over the years. Out of the 74 games between Pittsburgh and New York, though, three have been particularly noteworthy.

November 30, 1952

For the Steelers, you knew it could be a good day right from the kickoff. Or at least you could dream of it being a good day. Indeed, when Lynn Chandnois took the opening kick 91 yards for a touchdown, you could overlook the fact that it was the same old Steelers after all, a team that opened the season with four losses and was taking a 3–6 record into the contest against the first-place Giants.

Behind four Jim Finks touchdown passes and 123 yards rushing by rookie fullback Ed "Mighty Mo" Modzelewski, the Steelers crushed the Giants, 63–7, at Forbes Field for the most lopsided win in Pittsburgh and the most lopsided loss in Giants history.

Along the way, the Giants lost their first two quarterbacks, Charley Conerly and Fred Benners, and had to rely on defensive starter Tom Landry.

The Steelers set nine single-game or season records in that game.

December 15, 1963

It was one of those rare times in the 1960s when the Steelers were pretty good. They headed into the final game of the 1963 season with a chance to go to the playoffs. Sitting at 7–3–3, all they had to do was beat the Giants in New York in the season

ISN'T THAT WHY THEY CALL IT A HOME-FIELD ADVANTAGE?

The Steelers had a little problem with the Heinz Field playing surface before and during the Miami game in 2007 (as if you could have forgotten about that game). After a weekend that included high school games on Friday and a Pitt game on Saturday, Heinz Field officials decided to change the turf in time for the Steelers' game that Monday night. Of course, it rained and rained and the surface didn't take. Although the grass held up during the next home game against Cincinnati, it wasn't free from criticism.

Four days before the Steelers played host to Jacksonville in a 2007 AFC wild-card game, Jacksonville running back Fred Taylor wasn't worried about the Terrible Towels. He was concerned about the "terrible" turf.

"That field is terrible," said Taylor, who rushed for 147 yards and the winning touchdown at Heinz Field about three weeks earlier in Jacksonville's 29–22 victory. No other opposing runner hit the century mark in yards at Heinz Field during the season.

No matter to Taylor.

"That's a lawsuit pending," he said of the field. "That's ridiculous."

In that regular-season game between the teams, on a snowy field, the Jaguars from Florida, the only visiting team to win at Heinz during 2007, out-rushed the Steelers 224–115 and gained more overall yardage by a 421–217 margin.

Taylor, who said he prefers grass, suggested the Steelers put up $1 million to switch from grass to artificial turf, especially if they're going to allow high school and Pitt games to be played there.

"It just goes completely bad," he said. "So I think a million-dollar investment won't hurt their pockets."

Well, it might not suit the Steeler players that well. To a man, they say they prefer the current grass field.

"They play on it," Taylor said. "That's their home field and they like to get down and dirty and play a physical football game."

Yes, Fred Taylor, that's why it's called a home-field advantage. Unfortunately, the home field didn't work this time. The Jaguars won the 2007 AFC wild-card game, 31–29.

THE STEELERS' COLDEST GAMES

Date	Opponent	W/L	Score	Temp.
Dec. 10, 1977	at Cincinnati	L	17–10	2°F
Dec. 17, 1989	vs. New England	W	28–10	5°F
Jan. 23, 2005*	vs. New England	L	41–27	11°F
Jan. 4, 1976*	vs. Oakland	W	16–10	16°F
Dec. 7, 2006	vs. Cleveland	W	27–7	20°F
Dec. 30, 2001	at Cincinnati	L	26–23 OT	20°F
Dec. 18, 1983	at Cleveland	L	30–17	20°F

* playoff game

finale. It seemed easy enough, considering they crushed the Giants earlier in the season, 31–0.

In a famous article for *True* magazine, Pittsburgh icon Myron Cope offered his assessment of what happened. "To the utter dismay of those who know their Steelers best, quarterback [Ed] Brown, a strapping former marine buck sergeant, took the big game too seriously," Cope wrote in the September 1964 issue of the magazine. "On the Wednesday preceding the showdown battle, he disappeared from his favorite saloon. He went into training.

"Now Brownie is not the kind of guy who has to dry out before a game. On the contrary, he is rather a high-class drinker, favoring liquid ensembles—for example, Scotch whiskey on crushed ice with a thin layer of Drambuie added."

The article goes on to point out how Brown, normally an accurate passer, missed his receivers through the whole game.

"Brownie had trained himself into the most miserable performance of his career," Cope continued.

In the third quarter, with the Giants leading 16–10, the Steelers' defense had forced New York into a third-and-16. One stop, that's all Pittsburgh needed.

"[Frank] Gifford caught a pass that picked up 30 yards, then they scored and put the game away," said linebacker Myron

Pottios. "I remember that play mostly. It was a tough catch, a one-handed catch on frozen ground. It was a great play on his part."

The Giants went on to win the game 33–17 and kept the Steelers away from the playoffs.

September 20, 1964

The game itself wasn't magnificent or important to the team's history. A photo from it, however, is one of the most famous in sports history. Aging New York quarterback Y.A. Tittle sitting on his knees, dazed, in the end zone at Pitt Stadium. His helmet is off, exposing his bald, sweaty head with a line of blood trickling down. Tittle injured his ribs on the play and was trying to catch his breath.

Steelers defensive end John Baker delivered the hit that left Tittle so pathetic looking. Tittle was scrambling and didn't see Baker come in with a forearm. The shot knocked Tittle's helmet off and jarred the ball loose. Rookie tackle Chuck Hinton picked it up and scrambled in for the score.

Pittsburgh beat the Giants that time, 27–24.

THE RAIDERS

As competitive as the Steelers' other rivalries have been, none were quite like the Oakland Raiders. During the 1970s, it was the greatest rivalry in the American Football Conference and one of the best in the NFL.

Through the 2007 season, the Steelers and Raiders have faced each other 23 times. Eleven of those occurred during the 1970s. Three times that game determined who would be going to the Super Bowl.

With the AFL-NFL merger in 1970, the Steelers and Raiders played once that season before the rivalry really took off, with two games in 1972, including the infamous "Immaculate Reception." Each game after that, both teams playing at a high level with great athletes, grew in intensity.

"After the Raiders there were no playoff games," Jack Lambert said. "Those games were honest-to-God kick-ass playoff games."

"We were so similar in people: a bunch of nasty guys that liked to play," he added. "And the great thing about it, after the

A HAND IN THE MERGER

In their own ways, rivals Cleveland and Cincinnati each had a role in Pittsburgh's move from the NFL to the new American Football Conference, when the American Football League and the NFL merged in 1970. The Steelers moved from the NFL's Century Division to the new AFC's Central Division. But it wasn't without a fight, especially from Dan Rooney.

The American Football League was seen as the "Mickey Mouse League." It was seen as more of a wide-open, renegade league, with offenses that weren't afraid to be a little innovative. It was a far cry from the old guard of the National Football League. Frankly, the higher-ups in the NFL, such as Wellington Mara, Vince Lombardi, and Tex Schramm showed an elitist attitude toward the NFL.

One person who wasn't as quick to dismiss the "other" league was the Chief. When it was decided that three teams from the NFL needed to move to the AFL, the AFL was considering Pittsburgh, Baltimore, and Cleveland. Art Rooney was willing to ponder moving to the new American Football Conference. His son, Dan, however, wasn't as open to the idea.

"I was totally against this," said Dan Rooney. "I didn't want the Pittsburgh Steelers to be one of the three teams to move over to the AFL. We weren't a second-rate team that could just be ripped out of the NFL.

"What would our fans think? We'd look like chumps, like the league's whipping boy."

When the owners met in New York, commissioner Pete Rozelle was so gung-ho that the three teams needed to move to the new AFC, he decided that the meetings would go on until the three teams had been selected. To make it a little more tempting, Rozelle said that the three teams that moved to the new AFC would receive $3 million, paid by the other owners.

Dan Rooney still wasn't ready to consider moving. After all, the AFL was the enemy. Merger or not, they were seen as the enemy. Cleveland owner Art Modell said that if the Steelers would be willing to move, he would move. Of course, that set Dan Rooney off.

"Dad put his hand on my shoulder and said, 'Danny, hold on. Let's think about this.'"

Dan still wanted to talk Art out of any possibility of moving when they went into Pete Rozelle's office. Rozelle handed Dan a piece of paper that read: "CLEV, PITT, HOU, CINCY."
They had their new division.

game Stabler would come into the locker room and we'd have a couple beers together. We hated each other on the field, but after it was over we'd say whoever wins, wins."

A great example of how heated—pardon the expression—the rivalry became, happened before the AFC Championship Game in January 1976 at Three Rivers Stadium.

The night before the game, now known as the "Ice Bowl" (although the Raiders might call it "Icegate"), there was sleet on the field. So the grounds crew put down the tarp and forced hot air under the tarp in an effort to thaw the field, or at least keep it from freezing any more in the minus-zero temperatures of the night. The tarp ripped overnight and the field near the sidelines remained frozen.

When Raider coach John Madden walked onto the field a few hours before the game, with the temperature around 16 degrees, the grounds crew was trying to melt the ice by pouring water on it.

"Here the field is frozen and they've got a hose out there and they're watering it down," Madden said. "I'm standing there watching them, and they're telling me they're trying to melt the ice! I said, 'Hey, it's so cold, it's going to make more ice!'"

Madden, as well as many others in Raider Nation, really felt the Steelers were trying to slow down Oakland's speedy receivers with the ice.

"I still laugh when I recall those Raiders' claims. After all, everyone in the league believed it was the Raiders who intentionally soaked their own home field week after week," Dan Rooney wrote in his book, *Dan Rooney: My 75 Years with the Pittsburgh Steelers and the NFL*. "We played on that same field. Our guys couldn't run on ice any better than theirs could."

Wasn't that the truth. Both teams struggled on the slick artificial turf that was made even tougher by a snowfall. The Steelers turned the ball over eight times, including two interceptions thrown by Terry Bradshaw in the first quarter. The Raiders weren't much better, turning the ball over five times.

"Cold as hell," Chuck Noll said, referring to the temperature and not his team's play. "You couldn't do things you do normally. You couldn't play perfect football, but it was a true test. It brings out character. Nobody wants fumbles, but you have to overcome them."

A 36-yard field goal by Pittsburgh's Roy Gerela accounted for all of the points scored during the game's first three quarters. But the teams combined for three touchdowns during a six-minute stretch in the final quarter. The first, following one of Jack Lambert's three fumble recoveries, came on a 25-yard run around the left side by Franco Harris.

On their ensuing possession, Ken Stabler and the Raiders struck quickly on six pass plays, culminating with a 14-yard touchdown reception by Mike Siani that cut the Steelers' lead to 10–7.

Then Lambert recovered his third fumble of the game at the Raiders' 20. On the next play, Bradshaw found John Stallworth in the back of the end zone for another Pittsburgh touchdown.

The Raiders stalled on their next possession, so the Steelers got the ball back with just a few minutes left.

But Franco Harris fumbled the ball and the Raiders recovered. Oakland got the ball to about the Pittsburgh 24-yard line with 17 seconds left on fourth down. Madden opted for the George Blanda 41-yard field goal, which cut the Steelers' lead to 16–10.

The Raiders recovered the onside kick but it wasn't quite enough. Time expired at the Pittsburgh 15-yard line after Mel Blount tackled Cliff Branch, one of Oakland's speedy receivers, who had completed a 37-yard reception.

Thanks again to another thrilling victory over their AFC rivals, the Steelers were headed to another Super Bowl. (There, in slightly warmer Miami, the Steelers would go on to beat Dallas in Super Bowl X.)

Even though the Steelers faced the Raiders three more times in the 1970s, including the 1976 AFC title game, that win over

Oakland in the 1975 AFC Championship Game marked the last time that the Steelers beat the Raiders during an era in which Pittsburgh-Oakland could be considered one of the best nondivision rivalries in pro football.

ROETHLISBERGER COMES UP BIG

The Steelers were overlooked throughout the 2007 season. With the likes of New England heading for an undefeated regular season, Indianapolis limping to victories with several starters hurt, plus the NFC storylines with Dallas and Green Bay, it was easy for the Steelers to go about their business quietly in 2007.

That is, except for a couple games in particular when Ben Roethlisberger lived up to the nickname "Big Ben." Coincidentally, he did it in back-to-back games, against two rivals: Baltimore on Monday night and then Cleveland six days later.

The weekend before the Monday night game against Baltimore had been huge. It was the reunion weekend for the 75th Anniversary celebration. The likes of Terry Bradshaw, "Mean" Joe Greene, Jack Ham, and Franco Harris were standing on the sideline. With the Hall of Famers watching, quarterback Ben Roethlisberger had a career night by tying the Steelers' single-game record with five touchdown passes. And he threw his in the first half. The other two quarterbacks who did that, Terry Bradshaw and Mark Malone, threw their five in an entire game.

In Pittsburgh's 38–7 win over Baltimore, Roethlisberger also threw a touchdown pass for a 13th straight game, breaking Bradshaw's previous mark of 12.

It was just one of those nights. Just like the good old days.

Roethlisberger, who hit Santonio Holmes for a pair of touchdowns in the first half, completed 13-of-16 passes for 209 yards.

And just so guys like Greene, Ham, and Mel Blount didn't feel left out, the Steeler defense forced four Baltimore turnovers—three of which were fumbles in the first quarter.

The win avenged the two blowouts leveled by Baltimore in 2006 by scores of 31–7 and 27–0.

Six days later, the Steelers played host to their old friends, the Cleveland Browns.

Even though the Steelers won 31–28, this one played out much differently than the Baltimore game. Pittsburgh swapped three Jeff Reed field goals for three Cleveland touchdowns. Not the best trade in the world, considering it put them in a 21–9 hole.

It was the Steelers' ninth consecutive win over the Browns. But it didn't come easily. Cleveland pressured Roethlisberger the entire game, forcing him to scramble and work for his two touchdown passes and one touchdown run.

The Steelers were trailing 28–24 in the fourth quarter when Roethlisberger manufactured a 78-yard drive that included two third-and-long conversions. One became a 20-yard pass to Heath Miller and the other a 10-yard run by Roethlisberger.

"All I ever hear is about [Tom] Brady and Peyton [Manning], but this guy we have here is very special," said defensive end Brett Keisel. "He makes plays those guys don't make and that's what makes him so special. He can get out of the pocket, he can create, he's a beast and we're glad he wears black and gold."

IN THE CLUTCH

CHRISTIAN "MOSE" KELSCH: THE TEAM'S FIRST CLUTCH PERFORMER

The lead of the story in the *Pittsburgh Post-Gazette* on September 28, 1933, described it best. "The man of the hour in Pittsburgh grid-iron circles this morning, the fair-haired boy whose name is on everyone's lips, is a gent who never trod a college campus, never cut a lab period or a quiz. The very latest hero of the pigskin world here-abouts is none other than Christian Kelsch, but to thousands of sandlot football fans throughout the Tri-State district, the burly Northsider is just plain Mose."

Indeed, Christian "Mose" Kelsch, who at 36 was four years older than Art Rooney, could be described as the first on-field hero for the Steelers. After all it was his play in that September game in 1933 that helped the Steelers erase a 13-point deficit and get the organization's first win.

After the Pirates lost the first game of their existence in a hapless 23–2 showing against New York the week before, the Pirates (and their fans) wanted a sign that this whole NFL thing would be good.

Things didn't look so hot early in the game against the Chicago Cardinals. On a rain-soaked field, the Pirates found themselves down 13–0 in the second quarter.

Midway through the quarter, Pittsburgh's Martin "Butch" Kottler picked off a Jim Bausch pass and returned it 99 yards for a touchdown. Even today, that stands as the longest interception return in franchise history. (The second-longest is 86 yards.)

Then, with less than a minute left, the Pirates tied the game at

BY THE NUMBERS

59:43—That's how long it took for a team to score during the Steelers' rain-drenched Monday night game against the Miami Dolphins on November 26, 2007, in Pittsburgh.

With 17 seconds left in the game, kicker Jeff Reed hit a 24-yard field goal, giving the Steelers a 3–0 lead and eventual win over the hapless Dolphins. It was the first time since November 7, 1943, that a game went that long without any points (a scoreless tie between the Detroit Lions and New York Giants). After delaying the start of the contest for nearly an hour because of lightning and heavy rain around Heinz Field, the Steelers and Dolphins played on a field reminiscent of a wet game in 1943—sod coming up, standing water, no lines on the field— instead of a game in Pittsburgh in late November.

The conditions were so bad this time around that the NFL decided to skip the traditional singing of the national anthem, which was scheduled to be sung by Motley Crue front man Vince Neil.

"Due to the severe inclement weather conditions that caused a delay in last night's game in Pittsburgh, a decision was made by NFL representatives at the game to shorten pregame warm-ups and other activities and kick off as quickly as possible for the benefit of the in-stadium fans and the teams," NFL spokesman Greg Aiello told the Associated Press the day after the game. "This resulted in the teams not being introduced and the national anthem not being performed on the field. This action was taken solely due to the severe weather and the condition of the field."

To make matters worse during the 2007 Monday night game, because of an already rough playing surface, combined with the high school state championship on Friday and a Pitt game on Saturday, new sod was laid down at Heinz Field less than 48 hours before the game...directly on top of the old sod.

Either way, even though it took nearly the entire 60 minutes of regulation, the Steelers came away with the 3–0 victory—the lowest-scoring game in *Monday Night Football* history—and the Dolphins remained winless (0–11) on the 2007 season.

Coincidentally, in 2004 the Steelers and Dolphins played in Miami on the night of Hurricane Jeanne's landfall in Stuart, Florida—about 100 miles north of Miami. The Steelers won that one too, 13–3, which was Ben Roethlisberger's debut as a starter.

13 with a touchdown on a pass play from Jim Tanguay to Paul Moss.

Again came Mose Kelsch, sans helmet, for the extra point. He booted it through, giving the Pirates' organization its first win, and a win in comeback fashion.

Kelsch spent two years with the Pirates, doing nothing but kicking extra points and field goals, which was unheard of in 1933.

In July 1935, Christian "Mose" Kelsch, 38, died in an auto accident.

1975 PLAYOFF: ARE THEY SHOWING THE GAME IN SLOW MOTION?

Looking at the score, 28–10, it's easy to assume it was a typical 1970s non-Raider playoff game for the Steelers. A ho-hum blowout, if you will. But that wasn't necessarily the case.

In fact, the Baltimore Colts led the Steelers 10–7 in the third quarter at Three Rivers Stadium.

That is, until Mel Blount stepped up for Pittsburgh. Regular Baltimore quarterback Bert Jones was hurt, so Marty Domres was in for the Colts. Trying to protect a three-point lead, Domres threw a pass that was picked off by Blount.

On Pittsburgh's ensuing play from scrimmage, Rocky Bleier went in for the touchdown and the Steeler lead.

Even though momentum favored the Steelers, the game wasn't locked up until one of the most memorable moments in Three Rivers Stadium history. With Pittsburgh ahead 21–10, with a little more than 10 minutes left in the game, Bert Jones came into the game and was driving the Colts down the field. They had the ball at the Steelers' 3-yard line.

With about seven minutes left, Jones had little time to react before he was sacked by linebacker Jack Ham. When Ham hit Jones, the ball popped loose. Fellow linebacker Andy Russell scooped it up around the 7-yard line and headed the other direction with it.

"We had a blitz called and the tight end was on my side," Russell said. "Jack Ham made the play of the game by stripping the quarterback. The ball just bounced right up into my arms. I thought to myself that they'll tackle me in the next 10 yards so I want to make sure I hold on to it. Both of my wrists were sprained, so I had

A HAND IN DESTINY

The Steelers have been among a few teams in the NFL that could have altered the perfect seasons for both Miami in 1972 and New England in 2007. And, coincidentally, altered Miami's attempt at a winless season in 2007.

December 31, 1972—Miami Dolphins—The Steelers were feeling a great high as they headed to their first AFC Championship Game after they had just won the improbable "Immaculate Reception" game over the Raiders in the AFC playoffs. Although many of the Steelers players felt the future looked bright in spite of the loss to Miami, Art Rooney wasn't so sure. "I always felt we would win a championship someday, until that Miami game," the Chief said. "That's the first time I ever really got to the place where I felt I might not see it happen. In fact, after that game I said to some of the fellows I loaf with, 'I'm getting old. I'm not gonna be around here much longer.'"

November 26, 2007—Miami Dolphins—There's a certain irony that became evident midway through the 2007 season. As the 1972 Dolphins were bombarded with questions about their feelings of the dominating New England Patriots of 2007, the '07 version of the Dolphins was going for a perfection of its own. A perfect winless season. The Steelers aided that by overcoming the quagmire known as Heinz Field on an ugly Monday night and escaping with a late 3–0 win. (The Dolphins went on to beat Baltimore two weeks later for the team's only win of the season.)

December 9, 2007—New England Patriots—As Jim Croce sang, "You don't tug on Superman's cape; you don't spit into the wind; you don't pull the mask of the old Lone Ranger..." And you don't mess around with Bill. Unfortunately, Steelers free safety Anthony Smith messed around with the Patriots and their coach Bill Belichick when he pulled a Joe Namath–esque promise four days before the matchup between the two teams in Foxborough. "We're going to win," Smith told reporters. "Yeah, I can guarantee a win." Oops. The 12–0 Patriots had been dominating throughout the season until two close games before playing the 9–3 Steelers. And before Smith's guarantee. After a close first half, 17–13 in favor of New England, the Patriots dominated the Steelers in the second half and went on to win 34–13. New England quarterback Tom Brady threw for 399 yards and four touchdowns, two of which were big plays against

Smith. On one, Smith went for a Brady play-fake, leaving Randy Moss wide open for a 63-yard play. The other? A 56-yard flea flicker to Jabar Gaffney, who had burned Smith.

"I think the read they did on those plays was because of what he said," Pittsburgh defensive end Brett Keisel told the *Pittsburgh Post-Gazette* after the game. "Maybe try and take a shot at him. Why not take a shot, you know? And the shot went their way."

a cast on them. I would've lateraled, but I couldn't because I didn't have the flexibility in my wrists."

Russell, who wasn't the most fleet-footed of the Steel Curtain linebackers, made it all 93 yards—with the help of a couple blocks from Donnie Shell and Dwight White—for an NFL-record touchdown that sealed the game for Pittsburgh. It remains the longest fumble recovery for a touchdown in playoff history. And the clock operator had to turn the hourglass only three times.

"I know all the jokes," Russell said good-naturedly. "Most elapsed time for a fumble return. Jack Ham was concerned they were going to call delay of game. Ray Mansfield said NBC was going to cut to a commercial. But I was exhausted; sucking wind.

"Hey, I consider myself a smart player. It was late in the game. Why not run out the clock?"

The 28–10 win over Baltimore set up a meeting the next week between the Steelers and the Raiders.

1979: WHAT A WAY TO START

Veteran Jack Lambert hadn't spoken to rookie kicker Matt Bahr. Not a peep. For the whole season, which at the time just entailed training camp and four preseason games. Still, three words in that first sentence help explain it: veteran, rookie, and kicker. Not to mention the Steelers were defending Super Bowl champs and had won three titles at that point. Veterans had even less of a reason to talk with rookies, even one as potentially important as Bahr.

Bahr was a sixth-round pick in 1979 out of Penn State, where

MOST CAREER FIELD GOALS IN NFL HISTORY

1. Morten Andersen, 540
2. Gary Anderson, 538
3. John Carney, 413
(through 2007)

he had set 11 records for the Nittany Lions during his career. The Steelers picked him as a possible replacement for Roy Gerela, who wasn't as sure-footed in 1978 as he had been in his previous seven seasons for the Steelers. In '78, although Gerela was nearly perfect (44-for-45) on point-after attempts, he hit only 12 of his 26 field-goal attempts (46 percent).

Bahr and Gerela both had their chances to take the job. Near the end of preseason, Noll made his decision. In a somewhat surprising move, he cut Gerela, who eventually spent that season, his last in the NFL, with San Diego.

It wasn't long before Bahr had a chance to prove Noll's decision right (or wrong).

The Steelers opened the season on September 3 on the road against New England, a team many had picked to make a playoff run and supplant the aging Steelers. It also happened to be one of three Monday night appearances for the Steelers that season.

Since both teams were near the top of the division, at least in perception, it shouldn't come as a shock that the game went into overtime with a 13–13 tie.

As kickers oftentimes do, Bahr is quick to point out that he's the reason the game went into overtime in the first place. After all, he had missed an extra-point attempt in the second quarter and his 42-yard try near the end of the third quarter fell short. Not exactly how he imagined his pro career starting.

"Announcer Howard Cosell had written my epitaph," Bahr said, "and said [everyone was] witnessing my first and last game in the NFL."

DID YOU KNOW...

The Steelers and the Denver Broncos played in the modern-day NFL's first regular-season overtime game? The two teams finished the sudden-death overtime period in a 35–35 tie on September 22, 1974

Although a typical Cosell overstatement, Noll still had to vacillate about what to do when faced with fourth down at the New England 24 on the Steelers' first possession of overtime. Should he have veteran quarterback Bradshaw go for it or send in the rookie kicker who had missed two tries already?

Jack Ham tried to make the decision easier for Noll. "Have faith in [Bahr]," Ham told Noll.

When the Steelers lined up for the field goal, the Patriots called a timeout, presumably to "ice" the rookie kicker, although it rarely helps. That's when Lambert, who was on the Steelers kick-protection team, decided to utter his first words to Bahr.

"We have all the confidence in the world in you," said Lambert, who walked back to where Bahr had been preparing to kick.

"Those words mean as much to me today as they did then," Bahr said for the 2000 book *Super Bowl Sunday: The Day America Stops.* "Lambert defined why that was such a great team and he was such a great player, teammate, and leader."

Of course, Bahr hit the field goal and gave the Steelers the 16–13 overtime win. The Pittsburgh victory also marked the 100th win of Chuck Noll's coaching career.

It might seem like an exaggeration—if not completely absurd—to place too much emphasis on the importance of that opening-game win on the 1979 season. Or on Matt Bahr's contributions to the Steelers. After all, the Steelers were defending Super Bowl champs and Bahr would play only two seasons for the organization.

However, later in 1979, Bahr's heroics would be critical once again in another important overtime contest.

A week after the San Diego Chargers whipped the Steelers, 35–7, dropping Pittsburgh to 9–3 and in a tie with Houston for the division lead, the Steelers played host to Cleveland. By the start of the game, which was the Sunday after Thanksgiving, the Oilers had taken over sole possession of first in the division by beating Dallas on Thanksgiving Day.

Trailing the Browns 30–27 with less than 24 seconds left, Bahr came on and hit a 21-yard attempt, his third field goal of the game, and helped send the game into overtime. After 14 minutes, 51 seconds of the overtime period, Bahr nailed a 37-yard attempt, giving the Steelers a 33–30 win.

As for the importance of the overtime wins against New England and Cleveland, Pittsburgh finished the season with a 12–4 record, one game ahead of 11–5 Houston and with the same NFL-best mark as San Diego.

The Steelers ended up beating the Oilers—who had defeated the Chargers in the playoffs—for the AFC championship and a trip to Super Bowl XIV, where the Steelers would eventually beat the Los Angeles Rams.

NUMBERS DON'T LIE [OR DO THEY?]

1976: THE GREATEST STEELERS TEAM EVER?

It's always unfair to place a tag such as the "greatest" or the "best" or any other overused expression that media types like to give certain teams and players. It seems even odder, considering Pittsburgh's incredible Super Bowl dominance, to say a team that didn't even reach the Super Bowl might be the organization's best ever.

But when it comes to the 1976 Steelers, calling them the best isn't far-fetched. At least defensively, it was the most dominating season ever displayed by any team.

After opening the season with a loss to the rival Oakland Raiders, in a game best remembered for the cheap shot that George Atkinson delivered to the back of Lynn Swann's head, knocking Swann out of the remainder of that game as well as the next two contests, the Steelers won just one of their next four games. They beat Cleveland in week two, but then lost to New England, Minnesota, and Cleveland.

The two-time defending Super Bowl champs were mired in a 1–4 season and held last place in the AFC Central. They also were suffering one of the injuries that would hurt them throughout the season. Terry Bradshaw missed four games during the season, plus half of four more.

So in the sixth game of the season, at home against Cincinnati, rookie quarterback Mike Kruczek got the start. Coach Chuck Noll didn't want the untested Kruczek to get fancy. He was

INCONSISTENCY IS THE WORD

Since Terry Bradshaw retired in 1983, the Steelers have struggled to find consistency at quarterback. Granted, it looks like they have it now with Ben Roethlisberger, but other signal-callers since 1969 have had good starts, too, only to flame out. Here are the top 10, plus Terry Hanratty, Bradshaw's predecessor.

Quarterback Career Records (since 1969)

Terry Bradshaw (1970–83)	107–51
Kordell Stewart (1995–2002)	45–29
Ben Roethlisberger (2004–07)	39–17
Neil O'Donnell (1990–95)	39–22
Bubby Brister (1986–92)	28–29
Mark Malone (1981–87)	21–24
Tommy Maddox (2002–05)	16–16–1
Mike Tomczak (1993–99)	15–12
David Woodley (1984–85)	7–6
Mike Kruczek (1976–79)	6–0
Terry Hanratty (1969–75)	6–11

to hand off to Franco Harris and Rocky Bleier. The Steelers racked up 201 rushing yards (and 52 yards passing), while giving up just 171 total yards, and beat the Bengals 23–6.

Pittsburgh wouldn't lose again during the regular season. The Steelers put together a nine-game winning streak. Long streaks like that aren't completely uncommon in the NFL. But the way the Steelers won is impressive.

With Bradshaw's injuries, the Steelers tried to control the ball and the clock more, which meant a huge workload for Harris and Bleier. The two backs ran for 1,128 and 1,036 yards respectively, becoming the second set of teammates in NFL history to each rush for at least 1,000 yards.

The most impressive aspect of the season, however, was the defense, which simply dominated. During the nine games, only one team (Kansas City) had more than 250 yards. The Chiefs had

Jack Lambert, shown here in a December 1976 playoff game win against the Baltimore Colts, was a key member of the 1976 Steelers defense that may have been pro football's best ever.

DID YOU KNOW...

That George Atkinson's hit on Lynn Swann in the 1976 season opener brought about a change in officiating? At the time of the hit in 1976, there were six officials on the field. Even with six officials, no one saw the Swann-Atkinson play. The game's referee, Jim Tunney, wrote in his book *Impartial Judgment* that when the crew watched the film of the game later they didn't feel Atkinson's hit was anything more than a hard football hit. They didn't feel that he was intentionally trying to hurt Swann. Regardless, during their meeting in the spring of 1977, the Competition Committee added a seventh official—the side judge—to games.

257, but the Steelers forced six turnovers that game. And Pittsburgh went on to win 45–0. That was one of five shutouts the Steeler defense threw that year. Five.

During one stretch, they shut out the Giants in New York, and then San Diego, and then the Chiefs. And then ended the regular season with shutouts of Tampa Bay and at Houston.

Detractors like to point at the "easy" Steelers schedule. Granted, the records of the teams the Steelers played in 1976 weren't the greatest. Not one of those five shutout victims had a winning record. But then again, the Miami Dolphins didn't play a particularly tough schedule when they went undefeated in 1972. You don't hear much about that. And you shouldn't hear much about the Steelers' schedule in '76.

Plus, with the exception of the expansion Tampa Bay team, all of those five teams won games. And they all scored points during the season. It wasn't as if each of those teams was inept against everyone else.

Frankly, shutting out five teams, including three on the road and doing it in two streaks, is an incredible feat in the NFL. Not only could they not score a touchdown, not one of those five teams could even kick a field goal. Additionally, during the Steelers' nine-

BY THE NUMBERS

0—The number of 900-yard receiving seasons for Hall of Famer Lynn Swann. This is a tough one for Steelers fans to understand, but many people feel Swann was selected for the Pro Football Hall of Fame because of his big Super Bowl performances. His career numbers don't make a good argument against that. Forget the number of 1,000-yard receiving seasons. The closest Swann came to 900 yards was in 1978, when he caught 61 passes for 880 yards. Otis Taylor, for instance, whom many argue should be in the Hall of Fame, had two seasons of 1,000-plus yards and he helped lead the Kansas City Chiefs to a win in Super Bowl IV. Art Monk, who had 50 or more catches in nine seasons and surpassed 1,000 yards five times, finally received enough votes for the Hall of Fame in 2008. But there is no taking away what Swann meant as a big-play receiver for the Steelers.

game winning streak, opponents *combined* for 28 points!

"I think the 1976 Steelers team was the greatest defensive team in league history," said noted football writer Paul Zimmerman, "if you just look at what they did. Bradshaw gets hurt and Mike Kruczek goes in at quarterback and they shut out, what, five teams? Look at some of the records at what some of the quarterbacks did against them. You see a lot of 5-for-19s in there.

"They had 10 out of their starting 11 who made it to the Pro Bowl," added Zimmerman, who called that Steelers defensive unit the "greatest collection of talent ever assembled." "And the 11th guy, the guy who *didn't* make it, was the most feared of all of them, Ernie Holmes."

In their first game of the playoffs, the Steelers had little problem getting past the Baltimore Colts. During Pittsburgh's 40–14 win, however, the Steelers suffered big losses on offense. Harris left the game with bruised ribs, Bleier sprained his toe, and the other running back, Frenchy Fuqua, pulled a calf muscle.

"We had been confident that we'd go all the way," said linebacker Andy Russell.

BY THE NUMBERS

5-1-3—An unlikely double play? Yes, but just as unlikely rushing numbers. In the 2004 season opener against Oakland, Jerome Bettis finished the game with five carries, one rushing yard, and three touchdowns. Incidentally, the Steelers beat the Raiders 24–21 in what started a 15–1 season for Pittsburgh.

Suddenly, the ball-control offense of the Steelers was missing three main components heading into the AFC Championship Game at Oakland.

The Steelers were forced to go with Reggie Harrison in a single-back set. Harrison, a third-year player out of the University of Cincinnati, had rushed for 456 yards on 103 carries in his first three seasons. In 1976, he had gained 235 yards. Not exactly what a team with eyes on the Super Bowl wants to see in the conference championship.

In one of their worst offensive displays of the season, the Steelers' offense was inept against the Raiders. The Steelers didn't even get a first down until there was eight minutes, 32 seconds left in the second quarter. During that drive, the Steelers got their lone score of the game when Harrison ran in for a three-yard score.

The Raiders, already up 10–0 when Pittsburgh scored, added another touchdown in the closing minute of the half and took a 17–7 lead into halftime.

The Steelers were shocked. After shutting down the Raiders' running game in 1974 and earlier in the '76 season, they figured Oakland would be throwing.

The Steelers went three-and-out during their first two possessions of the third quarter, and never challenged the Raiders. Oakland added a touchdown in the third quarter to cap off a 24–7 win.

"They fooled our defense," said Russell. "Our defensive strategy [at the start of the game] was a hundred percent pass. They wanted me to jam the tight end on first down. The Raiders came out running and ran the entire first half. We made changes at halftime, but then they came out throwing the ball every down in the second half. Sure, we had the injuries, but the Oakland coaches get all the credit for that win."

"[The 1976 team] was without question the best team we ever had, but we lost a couple guys and that was the end," said Hall of Famer Jack Lambert. "That'll piss John Madden off because he thinks he had the best team that year, but without question we were a great team. It just goes to show you, you never know what's going to happen."

It's easy to play the woulda-coulda-shoulda game in hindsight, especially for a team that won four Super Bowls. But the 1976 squad is comparable to the four Super Bowl teams, except for that ring.

"If we would have been healthy, we would have had three Super Bowls in a row," Harris said. "I felt no one was going to beat us. We were on a roll. The only thing I feel bad about in my whole career is not being able to play in the 1976 championship game. I mean, maybe we could've won six in a row. You never know."

JUST CALL HIM "SLASH"

If asked to name one player who has had the most intense love-hate relationship with the fans of Pittsburgh, a case could be made for Kordell "Slash" Stewart.

It's hard to tell what exactly happened with Stewart. It seems the Steelers never could figure out how to use him. Or did they actually get more out of his ability than what was there?

During his eight seasons in Pittsburgh, Stewart threw for the second-most yards in team history (13,328) second-most touchdown passes (70); and the then second-highest passer rating (72.3). He also had the third-highest number of rushing touchdowns (behind Franco Harris and Jerome Bettis) and the highest rushing average (5.16).

The Steelers selected Stewart as a quarterback in the second round of the 1995 draft out of Colorado. It was obvious from the outset that he could do it all. He had a relatively strong arm — albeit not always accurate—and he could run.

Kordell Stewart scrambles for a first down against the Buffalo Bills in an October 1999 game.

So offensive coordinator Chan Gailey developed an offense that would use all of Stewart's strengths. Stewart could be a regular pocket passer, or he could carry the ball as a running back, or he could slide over to the slot and become a receiver.

At first, it worked. Teams didn't know how to stop him. But if they just gave him time, he'd eventually stop himself.

His outstanding ability and frustrating play are best illustrated in two games during the 1997 season: an October contest against Jacksonville and then the AFC championship versus Denver.

When the Steelers played host to the Jaguars on October 26, they had won their previous four games. Their last loss happened to be at Jacksonville, 30–21.

Things didn't start off well for the Steelers in this latest game

TRIVIA

Only two Steelers have worn either 0 or 00. Who were they?

Find the answers on pages 165-166.

with the Jaguars, as they found themselves in a 10–0 hole. But they battled back en route to 439 yards of total offense, including 317 passing yards from Stewart.

His crowning moment, though, came in overtime. The Steelers had tied the game at 17 with 2:21 left when Norm Johnson hit a 19-yard field goal. Pittsburgh won the coin toss and quickly moved the ball to the Jacksonville 17-yard line.

Five minutes, 47 seconds into overtime, Stewart tossed a shovel pass to Bettis, who maneuvered into the end zone for the game-winning score.

That game turned out to be vital for the Steelers as they went on to win their fourth straight AFC Central title. After beating New England 7–6 in the divisional playoff game, the Steelers hosted Denver for a chance to go to the Super Bowl.

About five weeks earlier, Stewart played one of the best games of his career against the Broncos at Three Rivers Stadium. He threw for three touchdowns and ran for two in Pittsburgh's come-from-behind 35–24 win.

Stewart was exhilarating at times and downright maddening at others during the championship game. During the Steelers' final touchdown drive, Stewart completed seven straight passes. But then there was the stretch earlier in the game, during the second quarter, when he had four straight incomplete passes followed by an interception.

Ultimately, the interceptions are what got him.

Shortly before halftime, with Pittsburg leading 14–10, "Slash" launched a 35-yard pass to the end zone. It was intended for Yancey Thigpen. Only problem was that Stewart threw into double coverage with Steve Atwater and Ray Crockett surrounding Thigpen. Crockett came away with it. John Elway led the Broncos the other way for a go-ahead touchdown.

In the third quarter, with the ball on the Denver 5-yard line and the Broncos leading by 10, Stewart tried to hit one of his old college teammates, Charles Johnson, with a pass in the end zone. Johnson had three Broncos around him and linebacker Allen Aldridge intercepted it.

"He played great this season and he got us here," Thigpen said after the game. "He doesn't have to apologize to anybody. He's a great player, and he's going to be a great quarterback before his career is over."

Well, Pittsburgh fans never really saw that greatness.

Stewart was the team's starter in 1998, throwing for 2,560 yards and rushing for 406, but the Steelers went 7–9.

The next year, Mike Tomczak supplanted Stewart as the starter. Wanting to keep his young player's playmaking abilities on the field, coach Bill Cowher moved Stewart to wide receiver. The Steelers went 6–10. Stewart began the 2000 season behind quarterback Kent Graham, but eventually won the starting job back. In 2001, he led the Steelers to an outstanding 13–3 mark during the regular season.

"There are not a lot of quarterbacks who struggle and are moved to another position," Stewart told *The New York Times* late in the 2001 season. "I had shown I could play receiver in my first couple of seasons, but I thought that was behind me. When you go through that kind of embarrassment, you have to really be humble and just shut up and ride the ship somewhere in the middle or the back. I learned to do that.

"I had to realize that a lot of great things had happened for me early in my career and now I was being tested. I had to swallow it. I had to come out and find a way to enjoy the game again. And I had to decide in my own mind that I could only be held down for so long by any situation before I reached my destiny in football."

Much like he did in 1997, Stewart once again led the Steelers to the AFC Championship Game in 2001, this time against New England. And this time at the brand-new Heinz Field. It didn't change the disastrous outcome.

Much like he did in the 1997 AFC title game, Stewart threw three untimely interceptions in the Patriots' 24–17 win. The last came with less than two minutes left when he missed Plaxico Burress and the ball fell into the hands of Lawyer Milloy.

STEELERS IN THE PRO FOOTBALL HALL OF FAME*

Name	Steeler Connection	Elected
Arthur J. Rooney	Founder, Chairman of the Board (1933–88)	1964
Bert Bell	Co-owner (1941–46)	1963
Johnny "Blood" McNully	Player (1934, 1937–39), Coach (1937–39)	1963
Bill Dudley	Player (1942, 1945–46)	1966
Walt Kiesling	Player (1937–39), Coach (1939–44, '49–61)	1966
Bobby Layne	Player (1958–62)	1967
Ernie Stautner	Player (1950–63)	1969
Joe Greene	Player (1969–81), Coach (1987–91)	1987
John Henry Johnson	Player (1960–65)	1987
Jack Ham	Player (1971–82)	1988
Mel Blount	Player (1970–83)	1989
Terry Bradshaw	Player (1970–83)	1989
Franco Harris	Player (1972–83)	1990
Jack Lambert	Player (1974–84)	1990
Chuck Noll	Coach (1969–91)	1993
Mike Webster	Player (1974–88)	1997
Daniel M. Rooney	President (1955–present)	2000
Lynn Swann	Player (1974–82)	2001
John Stallworth	Player (1974–87)	2002

*As of 2007

The next season, Tommy Maddox won the quarterback job from Stewart. That would be Slash's last season with the Steelers. The team granted him free agency after the '02 season.

He spent one year with Chicago and then two at Baltimore, ending in 2005. All the while he held onto the dream of playing quarterback in the NFL, instead of being a versatile do-it-all player.

"The same things I've had struggles with, every other quarterback is having," Stewart told *Sports Illustrated* between the Chicago and Baltimore gigs. "Because I played the wide receiver position I will never lower my standards just to play that position."

IT AIN'T OVER TILL IT'S OVER

THE IMMACULATE RECEPTION

Okay, so you've made it this far in the book and you're wondering where it is. Where is *the* play in Steelers history? Well, here you go. In essence, the best is last.

It's arguably the most famous play—and the most controversial—in pro football history. Heck, it could be said that it's the most famous play in football history, period. Sure, there was the "Music City Miracle" in Tennessee's win over Buffalo in a January 2000 AFC wild-card game. There was "the Catch," when Joe Montana found Dwight Clark at the back of the end zone leading San Francisco past Dallas. There was the "Band" in the Cal-Stanford game, and famous "Hail Mary" plays, including a 75-yard pass from Kordell Stewart in Colorado's win over Michigan in 1994.

But they all are merely nice little highlights compared to the play that's been viewed, reviewed, and broken down as much as the Zapruder film—the "Immaculate Reception."

One thing that gets lost in the play is the importance of the game for the Steelers. Until that game on December 23, 1972, the team remained the "same old Steelers." They had played in only two postseason contests in their history before then—both losses, first in 1947 and then in 1962.

So the "Immaculate Reception" wasn't an unbelievable play by a superstar on one of the game's best teams. It was a freak play by a great rookie on a team that was still learning how to win.

After going 6–8 in 1971, the Steelers started to turn things

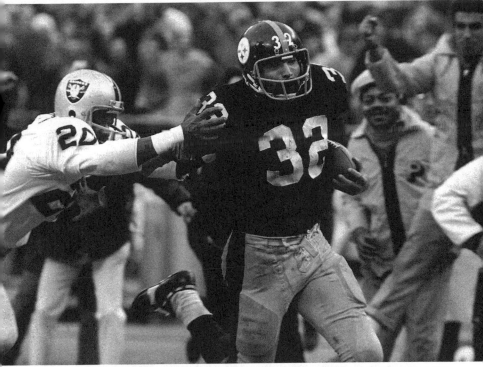

Franco Harris eludes a tackle by Jimmy Ware of the Oakland Raiders to score the winning touchdown in the AFC playoff game in Pittsburgh on December 23, 1972. Harris' "Immaculate Reception" came when a desperation pass to a teammate bounced off a Raiders defender and gave the Steelers a 13–7 lead with five seconds left in the game.

around in 1972. After opening the season with a win over Oakland in what started a good rivalry, the Steelers rolled through '72. They won 11 games and lost three, all three of which were on the road—at Cincinnati, at Dallas, and at Cleveland—by a combined 11 points.

It also was the first time in franchise history that the team finished with at least 10 wins.

Of course, their most remarkable game that year was the AFC divisional playoff game against Oakland at Three Rivers Stadium.

Even though both teams had good offenses that season (Oakland was third in the NFL; the Steelers, fifth), the game was a defensive grudge match. Neither team scored in the first half, and

SORRY YOU MISSED IT

Art Rooney had waited 25 years to see this: playoff football in Pittsburgh. The last postseason game the Steelers played at home was a 21–0 loss to Philadelphia on December 21, 1947. Even normally stoic reporters, now tingling from the Immaculate Reception, had to wonder. To see your team get its first postseason win—and to do it at home in the most unbelievable finish in NFL history—must've given you goose bumps, huh, Mr. Rooney?

It probably would have. If he had seen it. Rooney, being the kindhearted, warm owner that the players knew him to be, had left his suite during his team's last possession to head down to the locker room...to comfort the guys when they got there.

As one of the video specials from that game points out, when Rooney got on the elevator he was a loser, but when he got off he was a winner.

It must be true what they say: it ain't over till it's over.

the Steelers took a precarious 3–0 lead into the fourth quarter.

In the fourth quarter, defensive end L.C. Greenwood forced backup quarterback Ken Stabler, who had replaced ineffective Daryle Lamonica, to fumble the ball. The Steelers recovered. A few plays later, Roy Gerela hit a 29-yard field goal that gave Pittsburgh a 6–0 lead with less than four minutes to play.

But Stabler would get his revenge. On the Raiders' ensuing possession, Stabler moved his offense to the Pittsburgh 30-yard line. Then, with less than two minutes left, the Steelers flushed Stabler out of the pocket with a safety blitz and he started running toward the sideline. And running. Thirty yards and seemingly minutes later, Stabler was in the end zone. Just like that, the Raiders took a 7–6 lead.

When the Steelers got the ball back, Terry Bradshaw started off with two pass plays, the first for nine yards to their first-round rookie Franco Harris and then 11 yards to Frenchy Fuqua. Then they looked like the "same old Steelers." Three straight incomplete passes forced Bradshaw and the Steelers into a fourth-and-10

PLAY-BY-PLAY OF PITTSBURGH'S "IMMACULATE RECEPTION" DRIVE

Down	Ball On	Time Remaining	Result
First-and-10	Steelers 20	1:10	Bradshaw pass to Franco Harris for 9 yards
Second-and-1	Steelers 29	0:53	Bradshaw pass to Frenchy Fuqua for 11 yards
First-and-10	Steelers 40	0:37	Bradshaw pass to John McMakin broken up by Jack Tatum
Second-and-10	Steelers 40	0:31	Bradshaw pass to Ron Shanklin incomplete
Third-and-10	Steelers 40	0:26	Bradshaw pass to McMakin broken up by Tatum
Fourth-and-10	Steelers 40	0:22	Bradshaw pass to Fuqua broken up by Tatum; ball bounces into hands of Harris, who runs to end zone for 60-yard touchdown with :05 left; Roy Gerela kick

at their own 40 with 22 seconds left. They were hoping for a long play to get Gerela into field-goal range.

Then it happened. The Raiders forced Bradshaw to scramble toward the sideline. When his initial target, Barry Pearson, wasn't open, Bradshaw caught a glimpse of Fuqua. He let loose with one of his bullet passes.

You know the rest. According to Steelers fans—and logical physics—the ball bounced off the shoulder pads of Raider defensive back Jack Tatum, who was delivering a vicious hit to Fuqua, and Harris, who was charging toward the play, made a shoestring catch and started running.

"I didn't see the play," said Greenwood. "I was talking to the man upstairs. I didn't want to interrupt what I was doing. Next

DID YOU KNOW...

About 45 minutes after the game with the "Immaculate Reception," Franco Harris received a special telegram from Ol' Blue Eyes? It read: "The following is an order: Attack, attack, attack, attack." Signed: "Colonel Francis Sinatra (of Franco Harris's Italian Army)."

thing I know, the guys are jumping around and there goes Franco and I'm saying, 'Lord, I hope he has the ball.'"

Indeed, he did. Harris sprinted to the end zone, pushing aside one Raider defender at the 10, for the 60-yard touchdown.

Chuck Noll, who has since called that his favorite Steelers moment because it showed Pittsburgh was a "team of destiny," said, "Franco made that play because he never quit on the play. He kept running, he kept hustling. Good things happen to those who hustle."

To this day, more than 35 years later, it's unclear whether the ball bounced off Fuqua and into the hands of Harris, which was illegal at the time. Or if it went off Tatum first, which was legal. Or if it hit Fuqua and Tatum at the same time, which, according to the Steelers website, was legal in 1972. Regardless, it remains the most debated play in NFL history.

What happened over the next few minutes after Harris reached the end zone can be described with one simple word: chaos. Fans stormed the field. The coaches and Raiders tried to figure out what had just happened. It didn't matter to the Steelers. They mobbed Harris in the end zone. And the officials scrambled to make the official ruling, which included referee Fred Swearingen going to the baseball dugout to call the press box.

In the days after the game, there were several stories—especially in California—about why Swearingen called the NFL officials in the booth. At the time, there wasn't instant replay and booth reviews. Was he just looking for support? Did he want them to review the play on TV and make an unprecedented ruling?

In a story from the *Oakland Tribune* on Christmas Day, Raiders coach John Madden said, "The officials told me they didn't know what happened and they were going to check upstairs to see what it was. [Swearingen] went in to use the dugout telephone, and when he came out he called it a touchdown.

"I saw [supervisor of officials Art] McNally at the airport, and he told me there was no doubt. Tatum touched the ball. But then I saw Jay Randolph of NBC Television and he told me there was no way to make a positive decision off the TV replays."

The same article stated that Joe Gordon, the Steelers' public relations director, told reporters that day in the press box that McNally and the other officials watched the replay and then told Swearingen about it.

Of course, according to Dan Rooney in his book, *Dan Rooney: My 75 Years with the Pittsburgh Steelers and the NFL*, Swearingen might have been looking for some type of ruling from the booth, but he didn't get it. When the phone next to Rooney rang, he answered it to find out that Swearingen wanted to talk with Art McNally, then the head of the officials, who was at the other end of the booth.

Rooney writes of McNally, "He comes over, takes the phone, and I hear every word he says. The noise in the press box still hasn't died down, so McNally is pressing the phone to his ear so he can hear what Swearingen is saying. I don't know what the ref said, but McNally shouts into the phone, 'Well, you have to call what you saw. You have to make the call. Talk to your people and make the call!' Of course, no one had seen the television replay yet—it all happened too quick."

About that time, Swearingen huddles his crew on the field for a few moments. Then he steps away, faces the press box, and signals a touchdown.

"The press box goes wild," Rooney continues, "papers flying, reporters yell at each other—and I run for the elevator."

"Months later, I heard through a reliable grapevine that the day after the game, Frenchy Fuqua had a huge bruise on his left bicep," longtime Raider coach Tom Flores, who was one of Madden's assistants in 1972, wrote in the book, *Tales from the*

Oakland Raiders. "Jack Tatum was a hard hitter, but his shoulder wasn't the force behind the left bicep bruise. I looked at every film that I could get my hands on, and it was hard to tell."

As time has passed, the game has been remembered more for the bizarre ending than for its importance. After all, it was the Steelers' first playoff win. It was the game that many point to as the turning point for the organization; the one that helped them drop the moniker of "same old Steelers."

"Even though we lost the next week [to Miami], that win over the Raiders gave our club a tremendous boost," said cornerback Mel Blount. "We had a lot of important wins after that, but I think that one was the game that set the pattern."

1995: THANKFULLY, NOT AN IMMACULATE RECEPTION

Take your index finger and thumb and pinch a piece of paper between them. That's how close the Steelers came to a second straight disastrous end to the season in 1995. The previous year, Pittsburgh lost at home to an overmatched San Diego team in an AFC Championship Game for the first time since 1972.

The Steelers tried their best to repeat that performance in the '95 title game against the 11-point underdog Indianapolis Colts.

The teams swapped field goals in the first quarter, and Indianapolis added another one in the second quarter. Thanks to a slow-moving offense, the Steelers didn't take their first lead of the game until the closing seconds of the first half, when Neil O'Donnell hit Kordell "Slash" Stewart with a controversial five-yard touchdown pass, during which it appeared Stewart had gone out of bounds before he caught the ball.

The officials didn't call it and the Steelers took a 10–6 lead into halftime.

It was only breathing room. As had been the trend in each of the first two quarters, the Colts scored first in the third quarter on another field goal by Cary Blanchard. The Steelers added another Norm Johnson kick and were ahead 13–9 in the fourth quarter.

About halfway through the final period, Jim Harbaugh threw a 47-yard strike to receiver Floyd Turner, who was running down

DID YOU KNOW...

Myron Cope, who's generally considered the father of the term "Immaculate Reception," didn't come up with the phrase? According to the Steelers website, a man named Michael Ord first coined the phrase. The night of the game, Cope was at the WTAE-TV studios. "It was moments before Cope was to go on the air with his report of the Steelers' improbable triumph. A woman by the name of Sharon Levosky said that her friend Michael had a suggestion for a name for Franco Harris's catch—the 'Immaculate Reception.' Cope loved it, used it on the air, and the rest is history."

the sideline. With 8:46 left, the Colts had their first lead, 16–13, since early in the second quarter.

Steeler Nation was shocked. As Yogi Berra might say, it was déjà vu all over again. Would the Steelers lose at home in the conference championship two years in a row?

When the Steeler offense stalled on its next possession and had to punt to Indianapolis with more than six minutes left, things didn't look good. Starting from inside their own 10, the Colts got the ball to their 31.

On third-and-1, cornerback Willie Williams incorrectly blitzed, but he tackled Indianapolis running back Lamont Turner by the shoe tops in the backfield. If not for the tackle, Turner would have gained at least the first down and likely a lot more.

"I thought I was supposed to be," Williams said of blitzing, "but I got to the sidelines and found out it was the wrong coverage."

So the Steelers got the ball back with 3:03 left. For the most part, O'Donnell's mediocre performance had marked his day. The Steelers picked up a quick 20 yards on two pass plays, and then O'Donnell threw the ball directly to Quintin Coryatt—the Colts' linebacker. Ernie Mills batted the ball out of Coryatt's hands before the interception.

"I thought he had the ball and I just swung my arm and tried to hit it and knock it out," Mills said. "If he catches it, it's over."

Instead, the Steelers had new life. After an incomplete pass to Andre Hastings, Pittsburgh came down to fourth-and-3 with 2:25 left. O'Donnell found Hastings for a 9-yard play.

After the two-minute warning, O'Donnell threw a 37-yard pass to Mills, who made a wonderful grab, staying in bounds, at the 1. Two plays later, running back Byron "Bam" Morris barreled in for the touchdown and Pittsburgh lead with one minute, 34 seconds to play.

"We were hoping it wouldn't come down to what happened last year," said Steeler safety Darren Perry. "But if it did, then we were ready to make some plays so the same thing didn't happen again."

And boy, did they ever.

In the final 90 seconds, Harbaugh drove his team 46 yards to the Steeler 29 with a few ticks remaining. On the game's final play, Harbaugh lofted a high pass toward the end zone—the Colts' only real hope. As Ed Bouchette described it for readers of the *Post-Gazette*, "Indianapolis receivers and Steelers defensive backs packed into the end zone like bachelors waiting for the garter toss."

The Steelers' Perry and Williams touched the ball first before it hot-potatoed around several hands until the Colts' Aaron Bailey put nearly every body part on it as he fell to the ground. Then, seemingly in slow motion, the ball rolled innocently down Bailey's chest and onto the painted turf. Cornerback Randy Fuller helped it along.

Coincidentally, it was in the same end zone where Neil O'Donnell's pass didn't find Barry Foster for the AFC championship win against San Diego a year earlier.

"Maybe it was poetic justice," Bill Cowher, comparing the 1994 and '95 championship games, said. "Having been there again with the ball in the air and an opportunity to win a championship. Now I'm 1–1. It was a great feeling."

Bailey said afterward, "It was almost another Immaculate Reception."

Not this time. Luckily. Instead, the Steelers were headed to Super Bowl XXX.

TRIVIA ANSWERS

The Good

Page 11: Frank Parker, whom the Steelers traded to the New York Giants in 1969. Parker said later that season, "I'd have been mighty unhappy playing behind him. I've only got a few years left and I didn't want to spend them watching Greene become All-Pro."

Page 12: In 1976, 11 Steelers were selected for the Pro Bowl. In both 1979 and '80, 10 Steelers made the roster.

Page 16: On Wednesday, September 20, 1933, the then-Pirates lost at home to the New York Giants, 23–2. Incidentally, until Pennsylvania's "blue laws" were repealed later that year, the Pirates played their home games in 1933 on Wednesdays. Their first Sunday home game was on November 12 against Brooklyn. After tying Brooklyn in New York the previous week, the Pirates lost their first Sunday home game, 32–0.

The Bad

Page 28: One. In 2000, after finishing 9–7, the Steelers were shut out of the Pro Bowl.

Page 30: Pat Brady, who played for the Steelers during 1952–54. He booted an NCAA-record 99-yard punt for Nevada on October 28, 1950, in a game against Loyola-Marymount.

The Ugly

Page 47: The Jacksonville Jaguars, who beat the Steelers, 29–22, during the regular season on December 16, 2007, and then won 31–29 on January 5, 2008, during the AFC Wild-Card playoffs.

Page 50: On December 20, 2007, the Steelers beat the St. Louis Rams, 41–24. Interestingly, the Steelers didn't beat the Rams when the team was based in Cleveland before 1945, or in Los Angeles, where it was based through the 1994 season. (Unless you count Super Bowl XIV, which the Steelers won in Los Angeles, but not on the Rams' home field.) The 2007 season marked the Steelers' first trip to St. Louis to face the Rams.

The Super Steelers

Page 67: One. The only road playoff game the Steelers had to win before Super Bowls IX, X, XIII, and XIV, was the AFC Championship Game at Oakland on December 29, 1974. Pittsburgh beat Oakland 24–13, earning a trip to Super Bowl IX. Of course, the 2005 Steelers made up for it by winning three playoff games on the road before beating Seattle in Super Bowl XL.

Leading the Way

Page 88: The Steelers beat Cleveland, 16–13, in overtime on September 29, 2002, for Bill Cowher's 100th win.

Page 92: Atlanta, Baltimore/Indianapolis, Carolina, Detroit, New York Jets, and Tampa Bay never won at Three Rivers Stadium.

Heroes On and Off the Gridiron

Page 112: Five. Rocky Bleier, Sam Davis, Ray Mansfield, Andy Russell, and Bobby Walden made it from Chuck Noll's cleaning-house speech in 1969 until Super Bowl IX at the end of the 1974 season.

Numbers Don't Lie (or Do They?)

Page 153: Johnny Clement (1946–48) and Jack Collins ('52) are the only two players who have worn 0 or 00.

NOTES

The author would like to acknowledge the reporters and columnists who have covered the Pittsburgh Steelers since the team's inception in 1933. Much of their work has been referenced in the text of this book. Many of the quotations found in this book were taken from press conferences. The author has made every effort to note quotations that likely didn't come from press conferences, but rather from personal interviews. Also, all of the quotations in the book attributed to Rocky Bleier and Andy Russell were taken from personal phone interviews between those two Steeler greats and the author. Although noted below, interviews with other Steelers, such as Dwight White, Matt Bahr, and Woody Widenhofer, were taken from personal phone interviews between these men and the author for the book *Super Bowl Sunday: The Day America Stops*.

The Good
"When he was lucky..." *Steelers: The Complete History* DVD (NFL Productions, LLC, 2005).

"In those days..." Gary Tuma, "Steelers' Art Rooney in Retrospect," *Pittsburgh Post-Gazette* (August 26, 1988).

"For a period of years..." Vince Johnson, "Rooney Unique in Pro Football Hall of Fame," *Pittsburgh Post-Gazette* (September 7, 1964).

"When he shook your hand..." *Steelers: The Complete History* DVD (NFL Productions, LLC, 2005).

"Anybody that played..." *Steelers: The Complete History* DVD (NFL Productions, LLC, 2005).

"That man ain't human..." From Ernie Stautner's official website, www.cmgww.com/football/stautner/quote.html. Accessed 01-08-08.

"I didn't think..." Abby Mendelson, *The Pittsburgh Steelers: The Official Team History,* (Lanham, Maryland: Taylor Trade, 2006), 82.

"I was sure it was...." *The Sporting News* (December 20, 1969), 11.

"I'll take a punch..." *The Sporting News* (December 20, 1969), 11.

"That was the biggest defensive..." "Rooney Gets His Wish," *The Sporting News* (January 1975).

"While many of today's..." "In the Trenches," *Cigar Aficionado* (Winter 1995/96).

"I don't think..." Matt Fulks, *Super Bowl Sunday: The Day America Stops* (Lenexa, Kansas: Addax Publishing, 2000), 68–69.

"We were determined..." "Jack Ham," *Football Digest* (December 2000).

"The dynasty of Super Bowls..." *Steelers: The Complete History* DVD (NFL Productions, LLC, 2005).

"Rooney started his streak..." "Not Exactly a Novel Concept," *The Washington Times* (July 24, 2007).

"They were probably..." Jim Wexell, *Pittsburgh Steelers: Men of Steel* (Champaign, Illinois: Sports Publishing, 2006), 158.

The Bad
"We finally got..." *Steelers: The Complete History* DVD (NFL Productions, LLC, 2005).

"On a plane ride home..." Robert Dvorchak, "Steelers of '60s didn't win often, but the team was a-changing characters like Bobby Layne," *Pittsburgh Post-Gazette* (September 30, 2007).

"I was in Los Angeles..." Matt Fulks, *Super Bowl Sunday: The Day America Stops* (Lenexa, Kansas: Addax Publishing, 2000), 64–65.

"Sometimes it gets..." *The Sporting News* (November 29, 1969), 13.

"Losing was not something..." Abby Mendelson, *The Pittsburgh Steelers: The Official Team History* (Lanham, Maryland: Taylor Trade, 2006), 82.

"We were close..." Jim Wexell, *Pittsburgh Steelers: Men of Steel* (Champaign, Illinois: Sports Publishing, 2006), 158.

Arthur Jarrett story taken from Richard Whittingham's *Sunday's Heroes* (Chicago: Triumph Books, 2003), 123–125.

"Probably the best athlete..." Dan Rooney with Andrew E. Masich and David F. Halaas, *Dan Rooney: My 75 Years with the Pittsburgh Steelers and the NFL* (New York: Da Capo Press, 2007), 310.

"Rod is going into..." "Rod Woodson, Steelers' Longtime All-Pro Corner, Heads West," *The New York Times* (July 6, 1997).

"I think it's unfair..." *The New York Times* (January 8, 2003).

The Ugly
"The sight of Mike Webster..." Wright Thompson, "Steelers great Webster dies," *The Kansas City Star* (September 25, 2002).

"Mike would not accept..." Wright Thompson, "Steelers great Webster dies," *The Kansas City Star* (September 25, 2002).

"An aunt who was..." Leonard Shapiro, "After Football, a Tragic Freefall," *The Washington Post* (November 24, 2004).

Chapter 4

"Despite what a lot of people..." Matt Fulks, *Super Bowl Sunday: The Day America Stops* (Lenexa, Kansas: Addax Publishing, 2000), 61–62.

"They were just too good..." Larry Felser, "Dee-fense Tells Super Struggle Tale," *The Sporting News* (January 24, 1976), 9–10.

"I think a lot of us..." *Steelers: The Complete History* DVD (NFL Productions, LLC, 2005).

"When I think of Dallas..." Bill Chastain, *Steel Dynasty* (Chicago: Triumph Books, 2005), 131.

"In practices during..." Chris McDonell, *The Football Game I'll Never Forget* (Buffalo, New York: Firefly Books, 2004).

"Terry had called a play..." Chris McDonell, *The Football Game I'll Never Forget* (Buffalo, New York: Firefly Books, 2004).

"The hungry reporters asked..." Cliff Harris and Charlie Waters, *Tales from the Dallas Cowboys* (Champaign, Illinois: Sports Publishing, 2003).

"The referee or the umpire..." *Steelers: The Complete History* DVD (NFL Productions, LLC, 2005).

"They started controlling..." Matt Fulks, *Super Bowl Sunday: The Day America Stops* (Lenexa, Kansas: Addax Publishing, 2000).

"I never blocked a punt before..." "Back-to-back puts Steelers among elite," Labriola, Bob, www.news.steelers.com, accessed 12/21/07.

"I felt that we could..." Matt Fulks, *Super Bowl Sunday: The Day America Stops* (Lenexa, Kansas: Addax Publishing, 2000).

"I don't think we actually..." Matt Fulks, *Super Bowl Sunday: The Day America Stops* (Lenexa, Kansas: Addax Publishing, 2000).

Notes

"Any fool knows..." *Looking Deep*, Bradshaw, Terry and Buddy Martin. (Contemporary Books: Chicago, 1989) 48.

"Being called dumb..." Terry Bradshaw and Buddy Martin, *Looking Deep* (Chicago: Contemporary Books, 1989), 47.

"I can, too..." Terry Bradshaw and Buddy Martin, *Looking Deep* (Chicago: Contemporary Books, 1989), 124.

"As I sat opposite him..." *It's Only a Game*, Bradshaw, Terry and David Fisher. (Pocket Books: New York, 2001) 53.

"Bud [Carson] had us playing..." *Steel Dynasty*, Chastain, Bill. (Triumph Books: Chicago, 2005) 190.

"As strange as this may sound..." Matt Fulks, *Super Bowl Sunday: The Day America Stops* (Lenexa, Kansas: Addax Publishing, 2000).

"I didn't like the call..." Paul Zimmerman, "They Were Just Too Much," *Sports Illustrated* (January 28, 1980).

"The Pittsburgh team..." Bill Chastain, *Steel Dynasty* (Chicago: Triumph Books, 2005) 199–200.

"I didn't get the true extent..." Jerome Bettis and Teresa Varley, *Driving Home* (Chicago: Triumph Books, 2006), 141.

"I was screaming..." Jerome Bettis and Teresa Varley, *Driving Home* (Chicago. Triumph Books, 2006), 155.

"I was so open..." Len Pasquarelli, "Three big plays account for 155 of Steelers' 339 yards," www.espn.com, accessed 12/21/07.

Equal Opportunity
"Listen, we got to get..." "Sports of the Times," *The New York Times* (January 11, 1998).

"Later that day..." "Lowell Perry, 69, Football Star and Ford Aide," *The New York Times* (January 11, 2001).

Heroes On and Off the Gridiron
Much of Bill Dudley information from his "official" website, www.cmgww.com/football/dudley, accessed January 8, 2008.

"I thoroughly enjoyed..." Jim Wexell, *Pittsburgh Steelers: Men of Steel* (Champaign, Illinois: Sports Publishing, 2006), 4.

"The other owners..." Dan Rooney with Andrew E. Masich and David F. Halaas, *Dan Rooney: My 75 Years with the Pittsburgh Steelers and the NFL* (New York: Da Capo Press, 2007), 27.

Through the Draft: Good and Bad
"...too dumb to play..." Dan Rooney with Andrew E. Masich and David F. Halaas, *Dan Rooney: My 75 Years with the Pittsburgh Steelers and the NFL* (New York: Da Capo Press, 2007), 61.

"Buddy was going..." The *Kansas City Star* (October 28, 2007).

Browns and Giants and Raiders, Oh My!
"After the Raiders..." Jim Wexell, *Pittsburgh Steelers: Men of Steel* (Champaign, Illinois: Sports Publishing, 2006), 101.

"To the utter dismay..." Randy Roberts and David Welky, *One for the Thumb* (University of Pittsburgh Press, 2006), 96.

"Gifford caught a pass..." Jim Wexell, *Pittsburgh Steelers: Men of Steel* (Champaign, Illinois: Sports Publishing, 2006), 52.

In the Clutch
"I always felt..." Gary Tuma, "Steelers' Art Rooney in Retrospect," *Pittsburgh Post-Gazette* (August 26, 1988).

Numbers Don't Lie (Or Do They?)
"I think the 1976 Steelers..." Bill Chastain, *Steel Dynasty* (Chicago: Triumph Books, 2005), 146.

"If we would have been healthy..." Ed Bouchette, *The Pittsburgh Steelers* (New York: St. Martin's Press, 1994), 80.

"[The 1976 team]..." Jim Wexell, *Pittsburgh Steelers: Men of Steel* (Champaign, Illinois: Sports Publishing, 2006), 101.

It Ain't Over Till It's Over
"I thought I was..." Timothy W. Smith, "Waiting to Exhale: Steelers Win as Pass Fails," *New York Times* (January 15, 1996).

"Even though we lost..." Chris McDonell, *The Football Game I'll Never Forget* (Buffalo, New York: Firefly Books, 2004).

ABOUT THE AUTHOR

Matt Fulks, who started his journalism career while attending Lipscomb University in Nashville, Tennessee, after his baseball career was cut short by a lack of ability, spends his time as a freelance writer, editor, and co-host of a syndicated radio show, *Behind the Stats*. He grew up in Kansas City during the 1970s when the Chiefs were wretched. So, as most kids do, Fulks latched on to the best team he could like. Of course, in 1975, that was the Steelers. He's remained loyal to the Steelers since then. Today, Fulks is a regular contributor to various publications, including kcmetrosports.com—the website for Kansas City's all-sports TV station Metro Sports—and *The Kansas City Star* newspaper. He is the author/co-author of 12 other books, including *Echoes of Kansas Basketball*, *More Than the Score*, *The Road to Canton* (co-authored with NFL Hall of Fame running back Marcus Allen), and *Super Bowl Sunday*, for CBS Sports. More information is available at www.mattfulks.com. Matt resides in the Kansas City area with his wife, Libby, and their children, Helen, Charlie, and Aaron.